Winter Trails™: Wisconsin

"The perfect guide fo
prepared for their Wi
—I

"Phil Van Valkenberg
comprehensive, user-
country skiers and sr

Help Us Keep This Guide Up to Date

Every effort has been made by the author and editors to make this guide as accurate and useful as possible. However, many things can change after a guide is published—new products and information become available, regulations change, techniques evolve, etc.

We would love to hear from you concerning your experiences with this guide and how you feel it could be improved and be kept up to date. While we may not be able to respond to all comments and suggestions, we'll take them to heart and we'll make certain to share them with the author. Please send your comments and suggestions to the following address:

The Globe Pequot Press
Reader Response/Editorial Department
P.O. Box 480
Guilford, CT 06437

Or you may e-mail us at:
editorial@globe-pequot.com

Thanks for your input, and happy travels!

WINTER TRAILS™ SERIES

winter trails ™

Wisconsin

The Best Cross-Country Ski & Snowshoe Trails

by
PHIL VAN VALKENBERG

The Globe Pequot Press

GUILFORD, CONNECTICUT

Winter Trails is a trademark of The Globe Pequot Press.

Cover photographs: © Tim Jaman/Adventure Photo and Film; inset photo © Brian Bailey/Adventure Photo and Film
Cover and interior design: Nancy Freeborn
Trail Maps created by Equator Graphics © The Globe Pequot Press
All interior photographs by Phil Van Valkenberg

Library of Congress Cataloging-in-Publication Data

Van Valkenberg, Phil.
    Winter trails Wisconsin : the best cross-country ski & snowshoe trails / by Phil Van Valkenberg.
        p.   cm. — (Winter trails series)
    ISBN 0-7627-0599-X
    1. Skis and skiing—Wisconsin Guidebooks.   2. Snowshoes and snowshoeing—Wisconsin Guidebooks.   3. Cross-country ski trails— Wisconsin Guidebooks.   4. Wisconsin Guidebooks.   I. Title.   II. Series.
    GV854.5.W6V26   1999
    796.93'2'09775—dc21   99-39988
                                                                                CIP

Manufactured in the United States of America
First Edition/First Printing

To my daughter, Lily, who bounces back from a fall with a smile and snow on her face.

Wisconsin

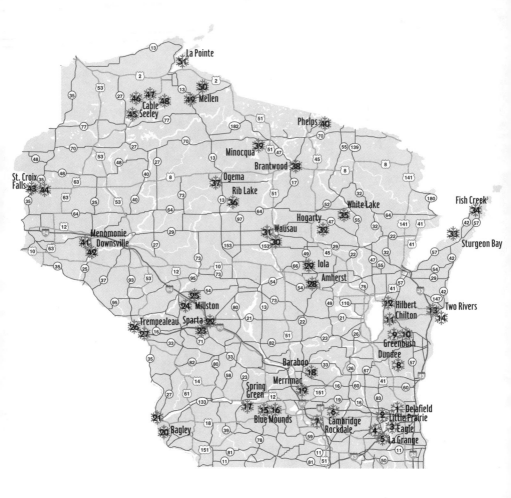

La Pointe
51

50

46 47 48
Cable 49 Mellen
45 Seeley

Phelps 40

Minocqua
39
Brantwood 38

Ogema
37
Rib Lake
36

Hogarty
White Lake
35
Wausau
31 32
30

St. Croix
Falls 43 44

Menomonie
41 Downsville
42

Iola
29

Amherst
28

Fish Creek
34

33
Sturgeon Bay

25
24 Millston

Trempealeau
26 Sparta
27 23 22

12 Hilbert
Chilton
14
13 Two Rivers

Two Rivers

9 10
Greenbush
Dundee
8

Baraboo
18

Merrimac
19

Spring
Green
17
15 16
Blue Mounds
7

21
20 Bagley
18

6
Cambridge
Rockdale

1 Delafield
Little Prairie
2
3 Eagle
4
5 La Grange

Contents

Acknowledgments

The quality and production of this book would have been impossible to achieve without the aid of many people. Much thanks to Paul Sandgren at the Kettle Moraine State Forest, Southern Unit; John Riley at Old World Wisconsin; Mike Bettinger at the General Store and Dale Carson, the mayor of La Grange; Ken Le Pine at Dane County Parks; Ron Zahringer at Ledge View Nature Center; Don and Donna Justin at Justin Trails; Marty Wacker at Portage County Parks; Dewey Ewers at Bear Paw Inn; Ann Dillon and Bob Rusch at Rib Lake; Jim Palmquist at The Farm; Dan and Lona Clausen at Minocqua Winter Park; Pete and Gail Moline at Afterglow Lake Resort; Doug and Jackie Kruse, Ron Bergin, and Gary and Sara Crandall in Cable.

Introduction

Winter is a magical time in Wisconsin. A day spent cross-country skiing or snowshoeing triggers something primal in us all. A feeling of well-
being comes from seeking harmony with the winter world. Whether the
day is sunny and mild or cold and windy, making one's way across
nature's snowy mantle is exhilarating. They say we humans evolved to
our modern form and intellect in the last great ice age. Perhaps that
explains it all.

The experiences of winter are all so tenuous. Snow or ice frosting on
tree branches can disappear in an afternoon. Pristine, sparkling, new
fallen snow will be different the next day. Wind-sculpted drifts are constantly changing. The unforgettable sight of a bald eagle swooping over
a river to pluck a fish doesn't happen every day. You have to be out in
winter to enjoy such wonderful sights. You can't get experiences like
these on video or the Internet, and you never will. They have to be lived.

Wisconsin has so many wonderful natural areas to explore on skis or
snowshoes. Two national forests, the Chequamegon (sha-WA-ma-gun)
and Nicolet (NICK-owe-lay) cover vast areas in the north. State forests
like the Kettle Moraine, Black River, and Point Beach are winter par-
adises. Devils Lake, Peninsula, Perrot, Rib Mountain, Interstate, Copper
Falls, Blue Mound, and Wyalusing offer inspiring scenery.

Trail systems at county parks and forests have embraced skiing and
snowshoeing. Standing Rocks, Calumet, and Timms Hill county parks
and Bayfield, Sawyer, and Marathon county forests are just a few. Pri-
vately run trail areas offer even more. Minocqua Winter Park, Bear Paw
Inn, Justin Trails, Catch-A-Dream Lodge, The Springs, Palmquist's The
Farm, and Afterglow Lake Resort are terrific destinations. At private
areas you may find lodging, dining, ski lessons, ski and snowshoe rentals,
clinics, and yes, even luxury.

Annual candlelight ski night tours at state parks have become very
popular. In a typical Wisconsin winter more than 150 ski or snowshoe
events are scheduled—Everything from cross-country and snowshoe
races and tours to clinics and swap meets. Events at the trails in this book
are always noted. Information contacts are mentioned in each chapter
and listed in the appendix.

There are more than 250 cross-country ski trail systems in the state
and countless snowshoeing possibilities. I have found the places that

offer something more—the best fifty-one trails. Places that have attractions like exceptional scenery, trailhead shelter, a commitment to cross-country trail grooming, good trail signage, and other amenities are described in this book.

Twenty-eight trails for cross-country skiing only are highlighted. I found fifteen trails exclusively for snowshoeing; an additional eight trails can be snowshoed and skied. Most trail systems and parks have an annual or daily vehicle parking fee or skier trail fee. The fees help maintain high standards; we should all be glad to support them with our dollars.

I have included detailed maps and trail directions, specifics on driving to the trailheads, and information on the amenities you will find at the trailhead and in nearby communities. The flora and fauna are described so you'll know what to look for. If I like a particular restaurant, I've mentioned it, and I never fail to let you know about places that serve a good microbrewed beer or ale.

All trails are rated for difficulty. I based this rating on what I perceived to be the abilities of novice and casual recreational skiers. Trails from easy to most difficult are included. If there are additional trails in the area, they are also mentioned.

Snow is the essential ingredient for all of this winter fun. You can count on abundant snow in the far north. Northern trails are likely to have more snow longer. March can be the most glorious time to ski or snowshoe in the higher latitudes. Southern trails get hit with wonderful snowfalls too. It is best to take advantage of this bounty as soon as you can. As they say: Get it before it melts.

Equipment

We can thank the Scandinavian settlers and Native Americans for creating skis and snowshoes. Early Norwegian immigrants mystified Yankee farmers by leaving strange tracks in the snow. Snowshoes helped native bands to weather the state's long winters. The wonderful Ojibwe snowshoe is a design attributed to the Ojibwe tribe, which has deep roots in Wisconsin.

In recent years, technology has changed the look and performance of both ski equipment and snowshoes. While there is much to be said for the beauty of traditional wood skis and wood and rawhide snowshoes, modern equipment has brought many benefits. The old stuff can still perform as well as it ever did, but the new gear may offer greater speed, lighter weight, traction or grip, durability, control, and safety.

Synthetic skis and poles have been available for decades. System boots and bindings, so called because they may not interchange with other brands, are well established too. Your first priority in selecting any of this equipment should be to find a good specialty ski shop that can fit you correctly and make sure you are getting the right stuff for your ability and desires. I can't emphasize this enough. Garage sale specials, hand-me-downs, and discount retail outlet packages have ruined the sport for a great number of people. Beginners usually think there is something wrong with them and give up rather than realize they made a purchasing mistake.

Fit is as important, or even more so, for novice touring skiers as for athletic experts. At least advanced skies know how equipment should perform and can likely modify their technique to make do. New skiers just flounder. Though skis pretty much look alike, they are not. The stiffness of the ski is of utmost importance for traction, glide, and downhill control. Specialty ski shop personnel can fit you by using stiffness gauges or doing what is called "the paper test." A boot with the proper fit and style is essential for comfort, warmth, and ski control. Poles, while less critical, come in a wide variety of types. Errors in fit will affect performance.

There are two types of cross-country skiing these days. Ski skating, in which the skis are worked with an angled, ice-skating motion, came on the scene in the late 1980s. The traditional ski style, very similar to the natural leg movement and arm swing of walking or running, is now called classic skiing. The majority of groomed trail systems in Wisconsin have some provision for skating. It is faster if done right, and it can be used on a lot less snow than classic. Classic needs more snow depth in order to have a set track, which helps greatly with control.

If you are a beginner, you should learn classic first. Well-fitted wax-less skis are viable options for classic. They perform best at temperatures around freezing (32 degrees Fahrenheit) and above. In almost all cases though, waxable skis are faster. Their glide performance increases greatly at colder temperatures. Remember that glide is the free part. It is what makes skiing more efficient than running. All accomplished skiers go for the best glide possible. For novices and casual recreational skiers, simplified wax systems make good performance easy to achieve.

If you have learned classic skiing, the transition to skating will be easier. You will have a feel for balancing on one ski, and you will have mastered poling coordination. It is easiest to learn skating on skis that are somewhat shorter than an advanced skier your size might use. Lessons are highly recommended with either technique. One session can get you started with movements you might never get or which may take years to learn. They say that muscle memory, the ability to perform a movement without thinking about it, takes about six weeks of practice to kick in. It is best to get a lesson at the beginning of the season to learn or improve your technique and ensure assimilation before the snow is gone.

Snowshoe choices used to be simpler. It was a matter of selecting from a few basic styles and getting a size about right for your weight. There are many more choices now, particularly with modern snowshoes. My definition of modern includes a metal or synthetic frame, a decking of synthetic material rather than the traditional webbing, and, most importantly, crampons under foot. Let me say right off the bat, if you are only going to have one pair, buy modern snowshoes. They may not look nice on the den wall, but the performance difference is tremendous in steep terrain or icy conditions.

I got my first pair of new snowshoes several winters ago. Fond memories of late winter outings in the Northwoods (yes, we do capitalize it here) on my now long-gone Alaska Trappers came rushing back to me. I also recalled how on any steep terrain I had to take them off and walk up. If there was a hard icy crust, the shoes would support me, but they were treacherous to control. The same went for lake crossings with windblown bare stretches. I wouldn't even bother going out in those conditions with my old snowshoes.

My modern snowshoes were incredibly light. They gave great floatation for their size, thanks to their sheetlike decking. The crampons, serrated metal grips on the bottom, performed several functions. The forward piece was articulated with the binding, so it rotated to a vertical position for maximum traction when striding forward. The heel pieces were aligned parallel and prevented the shoes from slipping sideways. I found I could securely negotiate icy stone or even wooden stairs with confidence. The compact size allowed me to sidestep. In deep, fresh snow, lifting them high to move forward was no problem thanks to their light weight. Wow!

There are advantages to traditional wood shoes, however. Well-crafted, natural material snowshoes can be quite light. A large snowshoe like the Michigan or Ojibwe will be very enjoyable on relatively level terrain with deep snow. The bear paw design is very tractable on

Cross-country skiing is graceful and exhilarating.

steep terrain. And traditional models with tails allow you to make a snowshoe chair. To enjoy one, find a sunny, sheltered spot, roll out your foam pad, and jam the snowshoe tails into the snow. Then just sit and do nothing but listen, dream, and feel the sun's warm rays. Crampon-equipped modern snowshoes don't offer the potential for this wonderful experience.

When buying snowshoes there are several things to look for with either type. Light weight is very desirable. You would be amazed at how sore you can get lifting snowshoes over and over again. Ounces matter. Don't assume that modern shoes are always light. The durability of heavier ones may be best for working or for true expeditions, but if enjoyment is your goal, go light. Many traditional snowshoes now have a neoprene webbing instead of rawhide. This adds durability and is maintenance free, but it also adds weight.

Friends and snowshoes go together.

Bindings vary greatly. Try them out in the shop with whatever shoes you have on. You can sit in a chair to put them on the first time. Do it again standing up and see how easy it is, then walk on the floor a bit. Because you will be putting on the snowshoes when standing outside, you want them to go on easily. If the shoes don't track well and fit tail to toe with your normal stride (nesting) on the floor they won't in the snow.

Poles are useful, sometimes necessary, equipment for snowshoeing. Usually any pole that is about the right size for classic cross-country skiing will be fine. Using one or two poles helps in negotiating steep terrain. As with snowshoes, light weight is important with poles too. A pole can do double duty by acting as a monopod to steady a camera. Some specialized poles are now available, including adjustable-length models, and more are sure to come.

The footwear you use for snowshoeing is important. Feet don't stay as warm as when skiing. A light, insulated hiking boot, the kind the makers of running shoes introduced, will be fine most of the time. On warm days, you can just go in running shoes. Again, lighter weight is an advantage.

Proper Clothing

We live in an amazing time. This is certainly true with regard to the variety of active sports clothing available these days. It is hard to recommend specific items, so for the most part this information is generalized. You'll often hear the term layering. It is key to comfortable outdoor winter recreation.

The layering concept involves dressing in layers, usually three or four. More layers may be used in extreme cold, but for freedom of motion it is best to go with four and vary the thickness of each item. The first layer should be thin and made of a wicking type of material. The idea is to move moisture away from your body and on to the next layer.

The second layer should be of a thicker wicking material to offer more warmth. For hard-skiing cross-country athletes, this layer may be a specially designed ski suit and the last layer needed. For recreational skiers or snowshoers, the layer might be a midweight shirt of synthetic material, combined with comfortable synthetic pants. One additional item of clothing for any man is a pair of windproof briefs. No explanation necessary.

For the third layer a synthetic fleece shirt or vest is ideal. A wool sweater is still a wonderful garment for this layer. You may want to choose stylish items for the third layer, as it will be what you ski or shoe in most of the time. The thickness will determine the warmth. For each outing select the garment for this layer based on the outdoor temperature. Keep in mind that snowshoers will want to dress more warmly than skiers.

The last layer is the outer garment, a long jacket, a short windbreaker jacket, or a windbreaker vest. The obvious function is to keep the wind from cooling your body. Here some type of breathable fabric is best. What is known as 60/40 poplin is still very good. Breathable waterproof materials, like Gore-Tex, are good for snowshoeing and necessary for either skiing or shoeing in a wet falling snow, rain, or drizzle. The material may not breathe enough for very active skiing. Some jackets are well designed with many vents, which compensate to an extent. A windproof vest may be best for active skiers. It keeps the wind off of the body core while allowing easy arm motion.

Many people ski or snowshoe in ordinary clothes, often made of cotton. This is fine for short outings at a trail with heated indoor shelter at the trailhead. For long trips in extreme cold at an area with no warm shelter, cotton can be dangerous. Cotton holds moisture close to your skin, possibly resulting in a loss of body core temperature. In a fall, cotton soaks up moisture from the snow. In addition to safety, you will be much more comfortable wearing wicking garments in the shelter or car afterward. If you don't want to completely outfit yourself, the best compromise is to get wicking garments for the first layer.

Wicking and breathability are important for caps, socks, and gloves as well. I think wool socks are still the best. I doubt there has ever been a better model than Wigwam's Innsbruck. Add gaiters for extra warmth and to keep the snow out of socks and laces. Baseball-type caps are fine for showshoeing, but may cause problems with seeing ahead when skiing. Chose headgear that covers or has the option of covering your ears completely. You can also bring a headband or earmuffs for this. Cross-country gloves need to be fairly light and flexible to allow efficient use of the poles.

Two other parts of your body in need of protection are the eyes and face. Light, comfortable sunglasses block out UV rays and prevent a brush with a trailside branch from becoming a serious eye injury. Yellow or orange lenses work well on overcast days. They allow you to see more definition in the snow. Though they are not often used today, scarves are wonderful for face protection. A long, loose-weave scarf is easy to breathe through and can be retied if it ices up.

Safety

There is an element of danger in anything we do. Injuries in cross-country skiing and snowshoeing are less likely than in many other active sports. At the same time, judgments you make and things you do in the way of preparation have a big effect on both the possibility and consequences of an accident.

Accidents can be the direct result of many factors. Among them are skiing or shoeing beyond ability, treacherous trail conditions, fatigue, getting lost, getting caught in the dark, and changing weather. These dangers can be prevented by using sound judgment.

California friends laugh at what a weather junkie I am. What they don't understand is that in Wisconsin the weather can kill you. Judgment comes into play in assessing the forecast and planning your outing accordingly. Remember, travel will be a lot slower in drastically colder temperatures or falling snow. Make a realistic assessment of your ability and that of your companions, especially children. Trails that are too long, difficult, or icy set people up for mishaps.

You may have your heart set on doing a 5-mile trail, but if your judgment tells you conditions aren't good, weather is iffy, or it is more difficult than you imagined, then attempt an easier or shorter trail. Remember that fatigue can take the edge off of ability.

The constant fight for control in icy conditions brings fatigue on sooner. Some things can be done to enhance endurance, like taking rests, eating energy foods, and drinking liquids. Remember that these also add to your trip time. If you started with just enough time to cover the trail at a steady pace, you could get caught in the dark. On any trip beginning in the midafternoon, it is a good idea to bring a small flashlight along. It will be difficult to read maps in the dark or as dusk deepens.

As a general rule, grooming on cross-country trails makes skiing safer. By making a smooth, consistent surface that a ski edge can bite into, grooming greatly enhances control on downhills and eases climbing. On the level, set tracks make skiing easier. All of this changes if a snowstorm blows in or wind drifts snow across the trails.

Even groomed trails can be as slick as a luge run if they haven't been regroomed after freezing. Some trails are groomed periodically rather than on an as-needed basis. At some trails, grooming is done only on weekdays. The ski area may have equipment to handle any situation, but if there is no one to use it on a Saturday night, Sunday skiing won't be good. Grooming is indicated in the at-a-glance trail information, under "Surface quality." If a trail is "groomed frequently," you can count on it being in good shape in just about any condition. "Groomed periodically" should alert you to use your judgment.

How well you ski affects safety. The most common novice mistake is to hold the pole incorrectly. You must pass your hand up through the strap loop and bring it down on the pole. Putting hands through the strap from the side sets you up for serious thumb injury in a fall. Your thumb can be trapped when your weight lands on a pole.

Take a ski lesson. The instructor will teach you how to hold poles correctly and use them to your advantage for balance and propulsion. You'll learn how to snowplow, that most important downhill technique that lets you control speed and easily handle turns. A first lesson will teach the herringbone, an

Skiing is a thrill a minute for kids.

uphill duck walk that lets you get over just about any hill. You'll even learn how to get up with minimum effort after a fall.

Everyone should be mindful of the condition of their equipment. Cracked skis, poles, or boot tips aren't likely to make it through a trip. Using Grandpa's wood snowshoes that have sat in the garage for years may get you just far enough to be in trouble. Leather bindings and rawhide webbing deteriorate over time. Test any old snowshoes in your yard first.

Items you bring along affect safety or the consequences of a mishap. A good-size fanny pack with an insulated water bottle holder is essential for all but the shortest, easiest, good-weather tours. Water keeps you hydrated, allowing your body to metabolize fat and keep its temperature up. Don't think it won't be needed in very cold conditions when you won't sweat much. On a cold, dry day 80 percent of your water loss will be through your lungs. Those steamy breath clouds are water.

A fanny pack allows you to carry an extra top or to stow the one you have on. A dry hat and gloves should be packed too. Extra warmth when needed can make a trek pleasant and safe. A mylar emergency blanket hardly takes up any space, and can provide essential warmth if a person is immobilized. Take along energy snacks for a carbohydrate boost when you need it, as well as ibuprofen and a basic first-aid kit. Ibuprofen can stave off cramping; a bandage over a blister can make it tolerable. Taking a first-aid course is a good idea for anyone. Don't be reluctant to ask passersby for assistance or to summon help.

Frostbite and hypothermia are potential winter threats. In extreme

Great grooming and beautiful scenery are standard for selected ski trails.

cold, wear adequate clothing, drink liquids, and keep your face and ears covered with a scarf or face mask you can breathe through easily. Frostbite prevention face creams are available, but a NATO winter warfare specialist once told me that natural body oils are best. Don't shave or wash your face before going out on extremely cold days. Signs of frostbite are white spots on the skin and loss of feeling.

Hypothermia is set off by a drop in core body temperature. Signs are loss of coordination, shivering, and disorientation. If you suspect a companion or skier you meet may be slipping into hypothermia use the finger test. Hold up two or more fingers and ask how many. Hesitating or answering incorrectly is an indication of trouble. Recognize hypothermia in yourself if your mind wanders or hallucinates.

Going out alone requires a few safety precautions. Tell someone where you are going and when you plan to be back, or at least leave a note on your car windshield. There is a big difference between going to a popular trail system and heading out on an isolated one. Obviously, at a popular area you are not really alone. Remember, though, that everyone will leave at some point. If you are out too late you could really be alone. Treat any trip to a remote area as an expedition. Be sure to be prepared for anything.

Navigation

The first navigation tip is: Stay on the trail. Leaving it adds time to your trip and getting lost is a real risk. On groomed cross-country trails accidental deviation from the route is less of a possibility. Still, consult your book map, "Directions at a glance," and any on-trail signs or maps. Trail marking varies from place to place. The type of marking you will find is indicated in "Directions at a glance." For simplicity, the maps in this book don't show intersecting trails; local trail maps usually do. Snowshoeing is more tricky. Often trails are less well defined and once someone strays, it seems that there is a trail there now.

It is not very easy to judge distances either skiing or snowshoeing. Checking the elapsed time and estimating distance based on your typical pace is one way. The "Directions at a glance" for a trail includes the direction a turn will take. If you have any doubt, check your compass (you did bring one, didn't you?).

Compasses are cheap. You can even get little ones that fit on a watchband. You don't have to be an expert with one, just know the rudiments. The compass arrow or dial will always rotate so that the N or red end of the arrow is pointing north. Face the direction of the arrow. Left is west, right is east and south is directly behind you. If you feel lost consult your map; use a flashlight if the light is fading (you did bring a flashlight, didn't you?). If you went east from the trailhead then you will have to eventually go west to get back to it.

In real emergencies a feature on the map, such as a nearby road, can offer the chance of assistance. Assess the wisdom of leaving the trail based on the distance, severity of terrain, and density of brush. Also note any streams that cross your prospective route. Leaving the trail is a more reasonable option on snowshoes than on skis. You can consult a compass almost constantly on snowshoes. If you want to reach a specific point, the trailhead for instance, build a direction error into your planned route. Don't go directly toward the point; travel in a direction you are certain will put you on the road or trail to the left or right of the trailhead. Then you know which way to turn to get to it.

GPS (Global Positioning System) is the coming thing. Small GPS receiving units can help you locate your position by analyzing the signals from three or more satellites. I used a GPS unit to help create accurate maps for this book. GPS can be an aid to navigation, but at present it has many pitfalls, and is no substitute for a compass. GPS units are complicated to use. They can be inaccurate in low areas surrounded by hills or in stands of evergreen trees. The unit may lose satellite contact, completely negating the value of the trip distance feature. The receivers are powered by batteries which drain quickly. A live compass beats a dead GPS unit any day.

Learn to interpret the topographic maps used in this book. If a trail runs parallel to the contour lines, it will be level or rolling. If it crosses contour lines it will be going up or down. The closer the contour lines are together, the steeper the grade. If you are confused at a trail intersection, this knowledge can help you choose the right direction.

Courtesy/Ethics

We often have a hard time imagining that we could offend anyone or do any damage skiing or snowshoeing. That is a mistaken assumption. Joint use of trails by skiers and shoers of different abilities complicates things. Since skiing and snowshoeing usually take place in parks, forests, or other natural areas, damage to plants and even animals is possible.

Staying on trails is the number one rule. Skiing or shoeing off trail can pack snow down on sensitive plants or even trap little critters, such as tunneling mice. What's more, your tracks are likely to lure others to follow, further increasing the damage.

Don't collect plants or tree bark, although something that has fallen or blown onto the trail is probably fair game. A little wind-blown scroll of birch bark that came off the tree naturally is a nice souvenir. Stripping bark off a birch can kill it.

Pay any required fees or be generous at donation boxes. It would be nice if everything were free, but trails take a lot of care and maintenance. User fees fund these efforts, keep the trails open, and make future improvements possible. Ski clubs often volunteer time to do trail work. Join one.

Most groomed ski trail systems don't allow snowshoeing unless separate trails are designated. Right now the state needs more designated snowshoe trails, but that is no reason to snowshoe on prohibited ski trails. On trails where joint use is allowed, snowshoers should travel well to the side and yield to skiers in most situations. Skiers are traveling faster and may not be able to stop or change direction easily.

Skiers have responsibilities too. On two-way trails travel on the right and yield to any skiers coming downhill. Alert skiers or snowshoers you meet by saying "passing" or giving a friendly "hello." Be sure you are in control of your speed. If you sense someone is having problems, pause and ask how he is doing. Offer to relay a message to any companions who may be ahead. If the skier is in real trouble, offer assistance or take the most direct route to summon help.

Trail Classification

The outings in the "Winter Trails" series are rated based on a three-tier classification system: easy, more difficult, and most difficult. I have tried to base this rating on what I feel are the abilities of the novice or casual recreational skier or snowshoer.

My rating may differ greatly from on-trail or on-map difficulty markers or notes. Many areas use the Cross-Country Ski Areas Association rating system. Its rating is always relevant to each particular trail system only. For instance, a green easy signed trail will be an easy trail for that area, but could be tougher than a most difficult trail at another area. I understand some of the reasoning behind the system, but feel it can endanger or turn

Solitude is part of the appeal of snowshoeing.

off casual skiers who end up on too-tough "easy" trails.

With my rating, you can count on an easy ski trail being flat or gently rolling. If a steep or difficult hill will be encountered, it is noted. Easy loops will be relatively short. An out-and-back trail may be longer, because you have the option of turning around at any time. Skiers with even the most rudimentary skills should be able to have a good time on these trails. All of the above applies for snowshoeing, except that more rolling terrain can have an easy rating.

More difficult trails require more skiing skills. Greater endurance is needed by both skiers and shoers. Trails will be longer and more rolling. Your general physical conditioning should be at a higher level. Skiing skills should include controlled snowplowing, snowplow turning, and herringbone climbing. Remember that icy conditions can move these trails into the most difficult category. For snowshoeing there may be a recommendation to use modern equipment with crampons and/or poles.

There are trails in this book that will challenge any skier or snowshoer. Some of the trails rated most difficult are as tough as any in the world. They should be avoided by anyone in icy conditions unless the groomer has the capability of "tilling," pulverizing the ice to allow controlled skiing. Most difficult trails will have steep hills and are likely to have tricky turns. Most difficult snowshoe trails may have snow- or ice-covered steps that must be negotiated. Modern equipment and poles are recommended.

Trail distances and cues are given in miles. Many cross-country trail systems show distances in kilometers on maps or trailside markers. A kilometer—a "K"—is 0.62 mile. A 3K marker indicates roughly 2 miles. Eight kilometers is about 5 miles, and so on.

Key to Icons

━━ cross-country skiing trail

snowshoeing trail

skate skiing (skating) trail

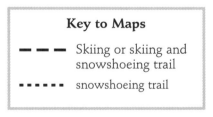

Key to Maps

— — — Skiing or skiing and snowshoeing trail

▪▪▪▪▪▪ snowshoeing trail

wisconsin

Kettle Moraine Lapham Peak Meadow Trail
Delafield, Wisconsin

Type of trail:	▬▬▬ ◄
Distance:	2 miles
Terrain:	Flat to rolling
Trail difficulty:	Easy
Surface quality:	Groomed frequently, double tracked, skate lane
Food and facilities:	Parking, enclosed heated shelter, hot chocolate and cider, and porta-type outdoor toilets are at the trailhead. Ski and snowshoe rentals are available at Lapham Lodge, a stone warming building up on the ridge, reached via the park road. Ski retail and repair are found at several shops in nearby Delafield, Oconomowoc, and Waukesha. All services are available in these communities. Delafield is fun for antiquing. Try Vinnie's for terrific pasta and pizza.
Fees:	A daily or annual state park pass is required to enter via car. Pay at the entrance booth when open or the self-pay station there.
Events:	Lapham Peak Nordic Ski Series, Wednesday nights in January and February; Candlelight ski tour, second Saturday in February; Lapham Loppet XC Ski & Snowshoe races, third Saturday in January.
Phone numbers:	Kettle Moraine State Forest, Lapham Peak Unit, (414) 646–3025; Oconomowoc Bureau of Tourism, (414) 569–2185.

If you are a weather junkie, a common skier affliction, Lapham Peak should be your mecca. The 1,233-foot ridge high point, the loftiest spot in southeast Wisconsin, was where Increase Lapham (pronounced LAFF-um) made his weather observations. He is considered the father of the U.S. Weather Bureau and is known to have made the first weather prediction. We can assume this was the first correct prediction, otherwise they wouldn't have named diddly after him.

Seriously though, Lapham's contribution was tremendous. In the mid–nineteenth century, storms generated in the west devastated Lake Michigan shipping. Signals he received from Pikes Peak in Colorado allowed him to warn the lake ports of drops in barometric pressure, the sign of building storms.

The Meadow Trail will not take you to the top, but two other trails — the 5.8-mile Kettle View and the 7-mile Moraine Ridge—will. They both

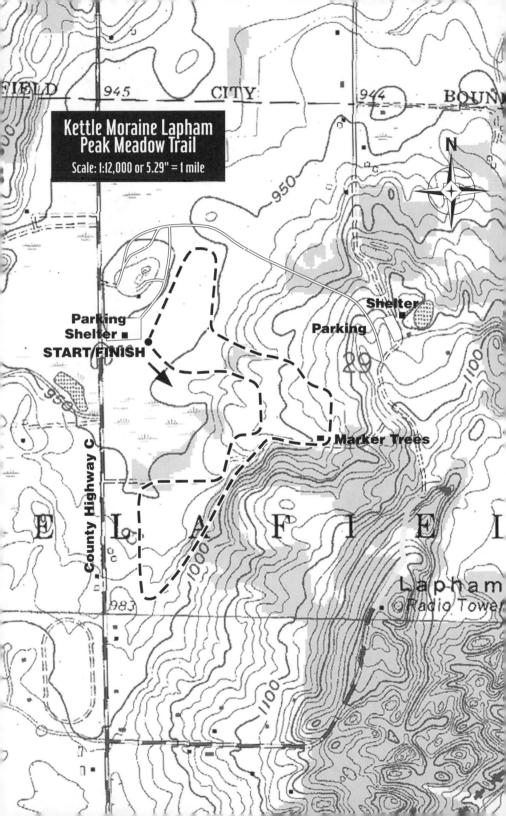

Kettle Moraine Lapham
Peak Meadow Trail
Scale: 1:12,000 or 5.29" = 1 mile

N

945   CITY   944   BOUN
FIELD
950

Shelter
Parking
Parking
Shelter
START/FINISH

29

Marker Trees

E   L   A   F   I   E   I

County Highway C

Lapham
Radio Tower

945
950
983
1000
1100
1100

return on the same screaming, 230-foot downhill run. I thought I'd go easy on you. Besides, Meadow Trail is lighted—you can make a night of it. Lapham Peak's staff has done a wonderful job with the trails, which are popular with all types of skiers. Good, dependable trail grooming is part of it. The wide trails leave plenty of room for anyone to maneuver. Double tracking on the lower trails means striders can ski side by side. The trailhead and ridge-top warming shelters make the area very hospitable. Another plus at Lapham Peak are snowshoe trails located on the west side of County Highway C.

The Meadow trail is wide enough for all types of skiers.

From the trailhead you'll ski counter-clockwise on the one-way trail system. Other trails will alternately split off and rejoin the Meadow Trail. Your ski begins with a slight uphill. It doesn't look steep compared to the ridge beyond, but take it easy and don't force cold muscles to strain up this 50-foot climb.

Turning south, there are several gradual downhill runs. They drop you back to base level before another easy climb. There is a long run down as the Meadow Trail splits off the route destined for the ridge top. On this downhill, watch out for skiers coming off the top and merging on the right. They may be breaking the sound barrier.

Directions at a glance

0.0   From the trailhead ski southeast.

0.8   Turn left (northeast) on the Meadow Trail (green) as the blue and black trails continue straight.

1.0   Continue straight (northeast) as the blue and black trails merge from the right.

1.4   Turn left (north) as the blue and black trails continue straight.

1.5   Continue straight (northwest) as the blue and black trails merge from the right. Follow to trailhead.

There is one more climb, followed by the biggest downhill payoff on the Meadow Trail. You ski steadily up as the trail turns east into the thick forest. Look for the two Native American marker trees at the first intersection where you turn north. These trees were shaped when young to mark foot trails. At the end of this short north leg through the pines, the Meadow Trail merges with the other trails as they come off the hill again. Watch for skiers on the right, but don't let them keep you from enjoying this easy 80-foot drop down to the open meadow.

How to get there

From the I–94 Delafield/County Highway C exit, go south 1 mile to the Southern Kettle Moraine State Forest Lapham Peak Unit entrance on the left.

Kettle Moraine McMiller Blue Trail

Little Prairie, Wisconsin

Type of trail:	
Distance:	6.2 miles
Terrain:	Rolling and hilly with very steep sections
Trail difficulty:	Most difficult
Surface quality:	Groomed, single tracked, skate lane
Food and facilities:	Parking at the trailhead. The heated warming shelter is open weekends and has a snack bar and indoor toilets. Basic services are available in Eagle, 3 miles northeast, including the nice Back Street Deli for good sandwiches, pizza, desserts, and coffee. For excellent dining check out Heaven City in Mukwonago, 10 miles east. Reservations are a must.
Fees:	A daily or annual state park pass is required to enter via car. There is a self-pay station at the trailhead sign board; you can pay in the warming building on weekends.
Phone numbers:	Kettle Moraine State Forest, Southern Unit, (414) 594–2135; Whitewater Area Chamber of Commerce, (414) 473–4005 or (414) 473–0520.

Life is full of strange combinations. McMiller Sports Center is a classic example. Some of the visitors come here to ski, some come to shoot firearms at targets. The two coexist pretty well, even though the difference in equipment and appearance makes an unusual picture. Skiers

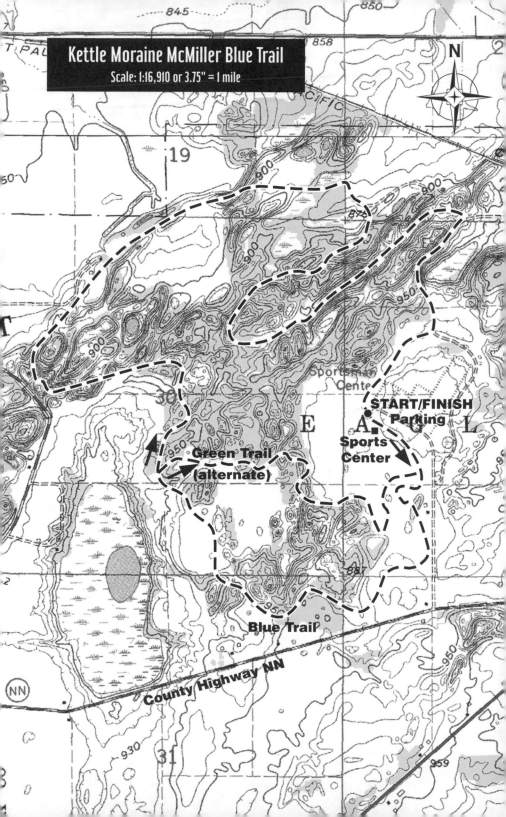

interested in the toughest trails in the Southern Kettle Moraine can't pass up the Blue Trail despite the crack of gunfire. In fact, when you are on the long last leg of the trail, after 4.5 miles without an inter-secting trail, the sound reassures you that you really will make it back.

The Sports Center warming shelter, open on weekends, is a pleasant place where you can get snacks or sit by the fireplace. There are always other skiers to swap tales of derring-do with.

The ski starts out easily enough, gliding through the pine forest over gently rolling terrain in a clockwise direction on the mainly one-way trails. After the first mile, when the Orange Trail turns off, things get exciting as you move into the upland hardwood forest. Steep, twisting descents and climbs in the 50- to 70-foot range are the rule. This is not a fun ski in icy conditions. Good downhill control is a must anytime.

After 0.5 mile of thrilling downs and lung-bursting ups, there is a break as the trail crosses open prairie. Then the excitement starts all over again, this time for nearly a mile. By then you'll have passed the turnoff for the 3.7-mile Green Trail, the last opportunity to shorten the trip.

Farther on, the Blue Trail goes by an old farm and cruises the flat on an abandoned road for 0.5 mile. Then you're in for more than 2 miles of ridge running, rocket descents, and turtle-pace climbs, as well as the toughest climb of the day, a seemingly endless 140-foot ascent. You cover the last 0.3 mile on blessedly flat terrain as you round the back

Twists, turns, and rolling terrain mark the kettle moraine.

side of the shooting range. Don't worry about stray bullets. High earthen embankments keep the lead under control.

How to get there

From WI 67, 2.8 miles south of Eagle, turn west on County Highway NN. Go 0.5 mile west to the Kettle Moraine State Forest; turn north into the McMiller Sports Center drive.

Old World Wisconsin Blue Trail
Eagle, Wisconsin

Note: Open only Saturdays and Sundays in winter.

Type of trail: ▬▬

Distance: 3.2 miles

Terrain: Rolling

Trail difficulty: More difficult

Surface quality: Groomed, single tracked

Food and facilities: Parking and ski rental are at the Ramsey Barn trailhead. Snacks, beverages, and indoor toilets are at the Clausing Barn Restaurant just north of the trailhead. Water and outdoor toilets are at the south end of the loop. All services are available in Eagle, 3 miles northeast, including the nice Back Street Deli for good sandwiches, pizza, desserts, and coffee.

Fees: A daily adult or child (ages 5 to 12) trail fee is charged.

Phone numbers: Old World Wisconsin, (414) 594–6300; Whitewater Area Chamber of Commerce, (414) 473–4005 or (414) 473–0520.

Internet: oww.shsw.wisc.edu

Want to visit New England, Germany, Norway, Denmark, and Finland all in the same day? No, I'm not talking about some jet set, trans-Atlantic Euro blitz. A pleasant few hours skiing at Old World Wisconsin State Historical Site will take you past reconstructed homes, shops, and barns of pioneer settlers from each of those homelands. The narrow, single track trails also give a feel for the past, so wax up those wood skis. A bowl of chili and a beer at the Clausing Barn Restaurant will top off the day.

The march of progress and the shrinking farm economy have taken their toll on many wonderful structures. In the mid–nineteenth century, immigrants flooded the state, spreading from Great Lakes ports to make new lives from the fertile land. The structures they built bore the character of their

Skiers pass a cozy-looking German half-timber house.

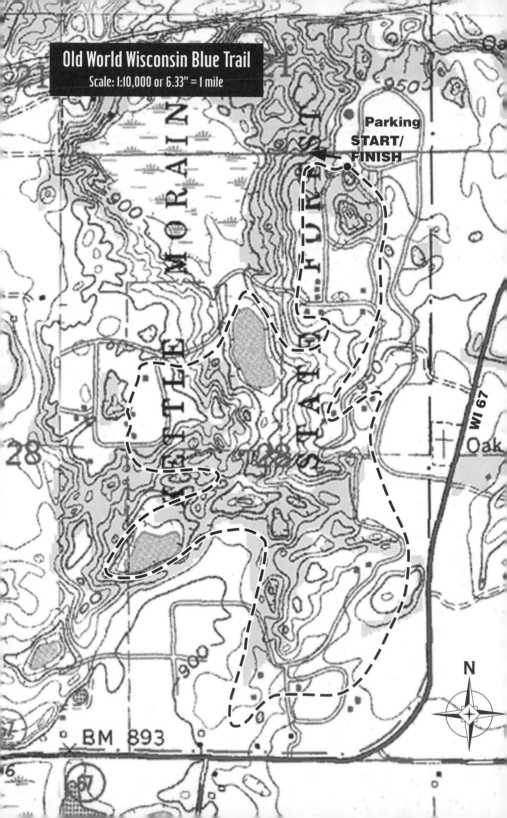

Old World Wisconsin Blue Trail
Scale: 1:10,000 or 6.33" = 1 mile

Parking
START/
FINISH

WI 67

Oak

N

BM 893

places of origin. Over the years many of these classic buildings were covered with clapboards, neglected, and sometimes abandoned.

The State Historical Society rescued and reconstructed buildings in the beautiful countryside at Old World Wisconsin. In summer it is a living museum, with authentically dressed people demonstrating everything from blacksmithing to polka dancing. Clustering all of these cultures here makes pioneer history accessible to the state's main population centers.

In winter Old World Wisconsin is quiet. The buildings are closed except for the Ramsey Barn trailhead and Clausing Barn Restaurant. This creates a wonderful experience of skiing discovery. You emerge from the forest to the sight of different communities as you follow the one-way loop in a counterclockwise direction.

The first architectural encounter comes just after leaving the Ramsey Barn trailhead. The trail passes the shining white Greek Revival buildings the Yankee New Englanders brought west as a hallmark of civilization. The style fell from popularity abruptly after the Civil War.

Directions at a glance

0.0   From the Ramsey Barn trailhead, go west on the Blue Trail, following the blue-and-white MORE DIFFICULT signs.

2.0   Continue straight (south) as the Black Trail merges on the right.

2.2   Bear right (east) as the Black Trail splits off to the left.

2.6   Stay right (north) as the Black Trail merges on the left.

The trail dips down 60 feet past a small pond before climbing up to the site of the German settlement with its warm, cream-colored, half-timber houses and barns. Another down-and-up run leads to the cluster of Norwegian log buildings, followed by a gently rolling stretch past Danish and Finnish structures. Each of these Scandinavian cultures brought its own distinctive way of shaping and joining logs.

As you return to the trailhead, the front side of the Yankee village will be in view through the trees, and you will have enjoyed an international tour for a fraction of the price of a plane ticket.

How to get there

From the town of Eagle, go south on WI 67 1.5 miles and turn right into the Old World Wisconsin entrance drive. Follow it to the parking area.

Kettle Moraine John Muir Orange Trail

La Grange, Wisconsin

Type of trail:	▬▬ ▭
Also used by:	Hikers
Distance:	4.0 miles
Terrain:	Flat, rolling, hilly with steep sections
Trail difficulty:	More difficult
Surface quality:	Ungroomed; skier, hiker, and snowshoer packed
Food and facilities:	Parking and flush toilets are at the John Muir trailhead on the west side off County Highway H. Parking and an enclosed heated shelter with water and flush toilets are located on the east side of county Highway H at the Nordic Ski Trails trailhead. Good food, microbrews, snacks, and ski and snowshoe rental and retail are found at the La Grange General Store, 2 miles south. All services are available in Whitewater, 9 miles west.
Fees:	A daily or annual state park pass is required to enter via car. There is a self-pay station at the trailhead sign board.
Phone numbers:	Kettle Moraine State Forest, Southern Unit, (414) 594–2135; Whitewater Area Chamber of Commerce, (414) 473–4005 or (414) 473–0520.
Equipment note:	Any type of snowshoe will do if used with at least one ski pole.

John Muir may have been Wisconsin's greatest gift to the cause of wilderness preservation. Brought from Scotland to the Wisconsin frontier as a child, he spent his youth and college years in the state. The changes he saw even then, as wilderness gave way to development, made him value the wild world of nature and he fought to preserve it. He was one of the founders of the Sierra Club and is considered the father of the National Parks system.

The Muir Trail is an appropriate honor for this visionary figure. Thanks to the Kettle Moraine

The woods are deep along the John Muir trail.

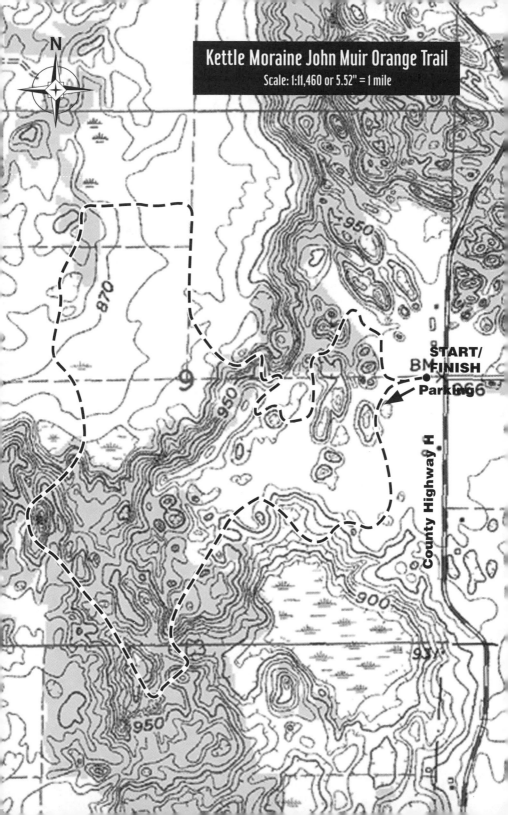

N

Kettle Moraine John Muir Orange Trail
Scale: 1:11,460 or 5.52" = 1 mile

950

870

9

950

START/
FINISH

BM

966

Parking

County Highway H

900

950

950

93

State Forest, a wilderness haven will survive the rampant development in surrounding Waukesha County. You'll understand Muir's appreciation of the importance of the wild country as you make your way through the unbroken snow on snowshoes or skis.

From the trailhead the clockwise loop first passes over mixed forest and prairie. Plunging into the deep oak and maple forest, it soon dips down and up the steep side of a huge kettle pit left by a glacial ice block buried in the earth. Then you are on roller coaster terrain—loved by the mountain bikers who flock here in summer—for the next mile. Along the way you will go retro (the wrong way) on a short stretch of trail marked DO NOT ENTER. Don't let this bother you. The one-way system is just for biker safety.

The trail emerges onto the gently rolling lowland, following old forest roads for a mile through plantations of pine. Then it is up, up, and away for a steady, twisting climb 90 feet up into the hardwood forest. From there it is an easy 0.5 mile ramble over rolling land back to the trailhead.

How to get there

From U.S. 12 at the crossroads village of La Grange, go north on County Highway H for 1.5 miles to the Kettle Moraine State Forest John Muir Trails parking lot on the left.

Directions at a glance

0.0   Go west from the trailhead sign board, following brown-and-white mountain bike silhouettes and color-coded posts. At this point posts include all colors; red, white, orange, green, and blue. Follow orange posts. YOU ARE HERE map signs are at most intersections.

0.8   Turn left (south) on trail signed DO NOT ENTER as the Red Trail goes right.

1.1   Turn right (southwest) uphill on the Orange Trail. This is also the Green Trail at this point.

2.4   Turn right (east) on the Orange Trail as the Green and Blue trails continue straight.

3.9   Stay left (east) and return to the trailhead.

Kettle Moraine Nordic Orange Trail

La Grange, Wisconsin

Type of trail: ▬ ◄

Distance: 3.1 miles

Terrain: Rolling, with some steep sections

Trail difficulty: More difficult

Surface quality: Groomed, single tracked, skate lane

Food and facilities: Parking and flush toilets are at the John Muir trailhead on the west side of County Highway H. Parking and an enclosed heated shelter with water and flush toilets are located on the east side of County Highway H at the Nordic Ski Trails trailhead. Good food, microbrews, snacks, and ski and snowshoe rental and retail are found at the La Grange General Store, 2 miles south. All services are available in Whitewater, 9 miles west.

Fees: A daily or annual state park pass is required to enter via car. There is a self-pay station at the trailhead sign board.

Phone numbers: Kettle Moraine State Forest, Southern Unit, (414) 594–2135; Whitewater Area Chamber of Commerce, (414) 473–4005 or (414) 473–0520.

The Nordic Ski Trails are originals. They were among the first cross-country trails in the Kettle Moraine State Forest during the boom years of the early 1970s and they are still terrific. The rolling kettle moraine gets a lot of the credit, as does the beautiful hardwood forest the trails wind through. The Orange Trail is actually the easiest loop on the Nordic Trails, but it is near the upper end of the more difficult range. If you find it a piece of cake, you might be ready for one of the other four loops. In any case, if you aren't an expert skier, ski these trails only in good snow conditions.

From the trailhead, the one-way loop system travels in a clockwise direction.

Fresh snow glorifies the oaks on the Nordic Trails.

Kettle Moraine Nordic Orange Trail
Scale: 1:10,000 or 6.33" = 1 mile

N

972

950

950

950

Underground

County Highway H

Shelter
Parking START/FINISH

BM
966

The excitement starts early as the trail twists around and up and down a series of craterlike kettles in the first 0.3 mile. This is followed by a break for 0.5 mile on an open ridge, although it may not be much of a break if the wind is howling out of the north. Next comes the most challenging downhill on the loop. A right, a left, a right, and you've dropped 80 feet.

The rest of the loop is more tame and you may be able to relax and enjoy the scenic woods. You can even reflect upon what an enduring gift to skiing the Nordic Trails are.

How to get there

From U.S. 12 at the crossroads village of La Grange, go north on County Highway H for 1.5 miles to the Kettle Moraine State Forest Nordic Ski Trails parking lot on the left.

Directions at a glance

0.0 From the trailhead sign board, ski north, following the Orange Trail markings on colored signposts. The Blue, Red, and Green Trails split off of and rejoin the Orange Trail. YOU ARE HERE map signs are at most intersections.

0.8 Continue straight (north) as the Blue Trail turns left.

1.0 Turn right (east) as the Blue Trail merges on the left.

1.2 Bear left (northeast) as the Red Trail turns right.

1.8 Continue straight (south) as the Green Trail crosses.

2.4 Continue straight (west) as the Blue and Green Trails merge on the left.

2.5 Turn left (west) as the Red Trail merges. Follow to trailhead.

Cam-Rock Park Area 2 Trail

Cambridge, Wisconsin

Type of trail:	━ ◁
Distance:	1.8 miles
Terrain:	Flat to rolling
Trail difficulty:	More difficult
Surface quality:	Groomed periodically, single track, skate lane
Food and facilities:	Parking and a porta-toilet at the trailhead. An open shelter is near the midpoint of the trail loop. In Rockdale, Heather's Place is a small tavern with snacks. The Night Heron Bed & Breakfast is popular for upscale lodging. All services are available in Cambridge: motels, B&Bs, a bakery, and several restaurants, including excellent dining at the Clay Market Cafe.
Fees:	A daily or annual trail fee is charged at a self-pay station at the trailhead. The annual trail pass is good at any other Dane County or City of Madison park.
Phone numbers:	Cambridge Chamber of Commerce, (608) 423–3780; Dane County Parks, (608) 246–3896.

Cam-Rock 2 is a short and sweet trail set between two picturesque small towns. The common thread between them is the Koshkonong Creek. A county park preserves the beauty of stream, marshes, and woods. Winter wildlife includes foxes, deer, and soaring red-tailed hawks.

Rockdale is about as tiny as you can get and still be a town. It makes up for a population of 160 with a charming collection of mid–nineteenth century buildings, including the still-operating mill and dam. There is a fine

Directions at a glance

0.0 From the trailhead follow the blue-and-white cross-country skier silhouette signs and arrows. Trails are signed for one-way travel in a clockwise direction, except for the initial 20 yards between the trailhead and the first intersection. Turn left at the first intersection.

0.4 Turn left into the pine forest. At this point it's possible to turn right and avoid one of the two somewhat difficult hills on the loop.

1.8 Go straight to return to the trailhead parking lot or turn right to ski another lap.

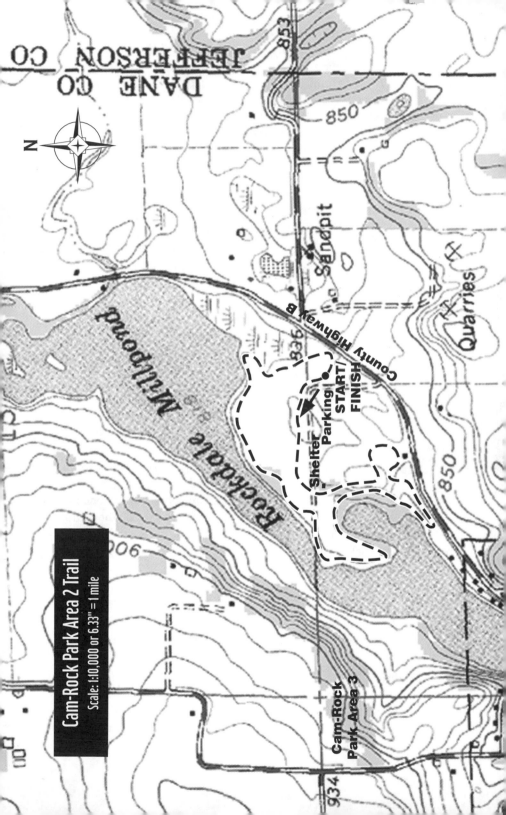

view of the dam from the County Highway B bridge across Koshkonong Creek. The broad millpond can be a great skating rink when the ice is good.

Cambridge has become a center for craftspeople and artisans. The famous Rowe Pottery Works, where reproductions of early American earthenware are produced and sold, attracts many visitors. The tourism supports a terrific bakery that serves lunch specials, and several restaurants. The outstanding Clay Market Cafe has a good selection of wines and microbrews.

The 1.8-mile Cam-Rock 2 Trail is at the very low end of the more difficult rating. All hills are in the 20- to 30-foot range. The clockwise one-way route begins with a moderate climb out of the oak woods to a nice overview of the park and creek. The run downhill is straight out and soon you are back in the woods climbing another 20 feet into a pine forest.

A prairie oak frames skiers at Cam-Rock Park.

The first tricky downhill comes as you leave the pines. It's an S curve that should be doable by anyone who can snowplow. Controlling speed will be important on the next, and only other, difficult downhill, which comes shortly after a steep herringbone uphill. This one is mostly straight, but it's on a side hill slope with a sharp left at the bottom.

The rest of the loop is a nearly flat cruise around a point and along the shore of the millpond. When conditions are right it is possible to ski the 0.1 mile across the millpond from the point to the ski trails at Cam-Rock 3. Any ice crossing is potentially dangerous, so only try it if you see other skiers crossing safely. Then follow their trail exactly.

The Cam-Rock 3 ski trail would have a most difficult rating, covering 1.1 miles and 150 feet of elevation. There is also a Cam-Rock 1 Trail, which you pass on the road between Cambridge and Rockdale. It is dead flat on an old railroad grade and can be taken 1 mile north all the way into Cambridge.

How to get there

From U.S. 12 in Cambridge, take County Highway B (Spring Street) south for 1.9 miles. Turn right (west) at the Cam-Rock Area 2 entrance road and park immediately on the left. The trailhead is directly across from the parking area.

Cam-Rock Park Area 3 Trail

Rockdale, Wisconsin

Type of trail:	🐾
Also used by:	Cross-country skiers on a short portion
Distance:	1.1 miles
Terrain:	Hilly with steep sections
Trail difficulty:	Most difficult
Surface quality:	Ungroomed, snowshoer packed
Food and facilities:	See "food and Facilities" on page 18.
Fees:	No fees for snowshoeing
Phone numbers:	Cambridge Chamber of Commerce, (608) 423–3780; Dane County Parks, (608) 246–3896.
Equipment note:	Modern snowshoes and at least one ski pole should be used.

Single track mountain biking came to Cam-Rock Park recently in the form of a gnarly (bike-speak), twisty, narrow trail that gets amazing linear distance from a very compact wooded area. Snowshoers have discovered the fun of tramping this little trail in winter.

At the trailhead you have a grand view of the Rockdale Millpond and the Cam-Rock 2 ski trails on the far shore. The slope in front of the shelter is popular for sledding. Kids can drop 100 feet if they don't get bounced off first. To get to the single track, you'll follow a groomed ski trail for a short distance. Snowshoeing on ski trails is not allowed, so stay off to the right side.

You'll turn into the woods at the mountain bike trail signpost and travel in a counterclockwise direction. The signs are on the opposite side of the post as you approach, but you can't miss them. From this point until you come out of the woods near the finish, you won't see any other formal signage. Unless the trail has been snowshoed, which is the case more often than not, it can be hard to follow in winter. When in doubt, look for colored plastic tapes tied to trailside trees. They were used to define the trail when it was originally brushed out.

The snowshoe trail crosses this pretty little glen twice.

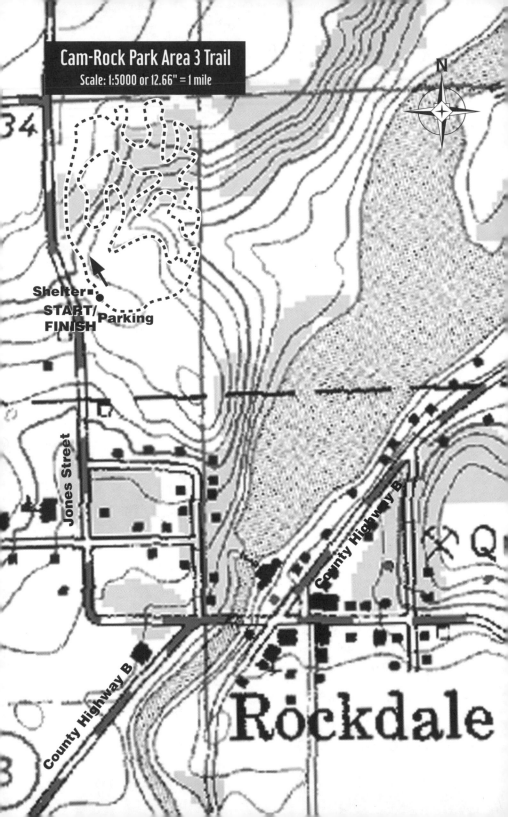

Cam-Rock Park Area 3 Trail
Scale: 1:5000 or 12.66" = 1 mile

N

Shelter
START/
FINISH
Parking

Jones Street

County Highway B

County Highway B

Q

Röckdale

34

3

In the woods you'll see why this is such a tough mountain bike trail. It snakes around, dips, crosses small fallen trees, and tackles steep ups and downs. You'll cover 120 feet of elevation. The loop is seldom level for more than a few feet. Halfway through you'll cross a lovely little glen twice. The rock shelves make a tiny waterfall if a big snowmelt is in progress.

Farther on, the trail swings through a little quarry then breaks out of the woods, but the tough stuff isn't over yet. You could bail out here; the mountain bike trail signpost is visible at this point. To complete the route turn sharply to the left and descend another short, steep slope. On the way down you can see a section of the trail already covered just a few feet away—what a tight system. At the bottom a right turn leads back out of the woods for a short run back to the trailhead. Look out for speeding sleds as you cross the slope.

Directions at a glance

0.0   From the Cam-Rock 3 parking lot, go north toward the open shelter 20 yards away. Go halfway around the shelter then follow the groomed ski trail signed WRONG WAY, by paralleling its route off of the right side.

0.2   Turn right (east) off of the ski trail at a post with a brown-and-white mountain bike silhouette.

1.0   Continue straight (south) as you emerge from the woods; follow mountain bike signs to the trailhead.

How to get there

From U.S. 12 in Cambridge, take County Highway B (Spring Street) south to Rockdale. As County Highway B crosses a bridge then bends sharply to the left (south) go straight (west) onto a village street. The street turns sharply north and becomes Jones Street. Follow it a short distance up a steep hill and turn right (east) into the Cam-Rock Area 3 parking lot entrance.

Kettle Moraine Zillmer Yellow Trail
Dundee, Wisconsin

Type of trail: ➦ ➧

Distance: 5.4 miles

Terrain: Hilly to rolling

Trail difficulty: Most difficult

Surface quality: Groomed periodically, single track, skate lane

Food and facilities: The Henry Reuss Ice Age Interpretive Center at the trailhead is open daily and has parking, water, and indoor toilets. Outdoor toilets are located at the south parking area off of County Highway SS. Dundee has several taverns with snacks. All services are available in Fond du Lac, 20 miles northwest, or West Bend, 20 miles south.

Fees: A daily or annual parking pass is required to enter via car. Pay at the Ice Age Interpretive Center.

Events: Candlelight Ski, first Saturday in February.

Phone numbers: Kettle Moraine State Forest, Northern Unit, (414) 626–2116; Fond du Lac Convention and Visitors Bureau, (920) 923–3010 or (800) 937–9123; West Bend Area Chamber of Commerce, (414) 338–2666 or (888) 338–8666; Ice Age Park and Trail Foundation, (800) 227–0046.

Although the Henry Reuss Ice Age Center doesn't acknowledge it, glaciers create great skiing terrain. I guess the center focuses more on teaching the fascinating story of the advance and retreat of the Wisconsin glacier than tooting the skiing horn.

The massive continental ice sheet was named after Wisconsin because early scientific studies of the phenomenon were conducted here. The fact that vast areas of land had been shaped by ice was a major discovery in the nineteenth century. Before, such areas were a puzzlement to the learned and a thing of folklore to the masses.

Henry Reuss was a Wisconsin congressman who was the prime mover in creating the

A glorious ski through snow-laden evergreeens.

Directions at a glance

0.0 From the southwest end of the Ice Age Interpretive Center parking lot, follow a short two-way spur trail marked with yellow-topped signposts to the southwest.

0.05 Turn right (west) at a "T" intersection and follow yellow-topped posts. This is a one-way trail. YOU ARE HERE map signs are at many intersections.

0.9 Continue straight (south) as the Red Trail, signed DO NOT ENTER, merges from the left. Signposts now have yellow tops with a red stripe below.

0.95 Turn right (west) following yellow-topped posts as the Red Trail continues straight.

2.9 Turn right (east) as the Red/Green Trail merges from the left. Signposts now have yellow tops with red and green stripes below.

4.0 Turn right (east) as the Red/Green Trail splits off to the left. Follow yellow-topped posts.

5.35 Turn right (northeast) on the two-way spur trail back to the trailhead.

Ice Age Trail. He loved the rugged terrain for its beauty. In his book *On the Trail of the Ice Age,* he says the area is a priceless haven for flora and fauna. Skiers would just say, "Yahoo."

Get ready to take on some tough kettle moraine terrain on the yellow trail. The biggest downhill challenge comes at the very beginning. Right after you join the one-way counterclockwise trail, you'll drop 100 feet in a 0.25 mile as the trail snakes down a steep glacial ridge. Soon you will be rolling through stands of red oak, sugar maple, and jack pine on an undulating surface that isn't nearly as tough.

A third of the way through, the trail snakes up and down a 60-foot-high ridge, followed by some easy cruising through a red pine plantation near the south parking area. Then the tough climbing begins as you scale the mile-long ridge leading to the trailhead. Stop a moment along the ridge at a scenic overlook of the valley below. In the distance to the left stands the Dundee Kame, conelike hill formed by waterfalls inside the giant ice sheet.

How to get there

From U.S. 41, take WI 67 14 miles east to the Henry Reuss Ice Age Interpretive Center. Turn right into parking area.

Kettle Moraine Greenbush Purple Trail
Greenbush, Wisconsin

Type of trail: ➤ ➤

Also used by: Snowmobiles and horses may cross the ski trails

Distance: 5.1 miles

Terrain: Rolling

Trail difficulty: More difficult

Surface quality: Groomed, single track, skate lane

Food and facilities: An enclosed heated shelter at the trailhead parking lot is always open. Fairly well maintained men's and women's outdoor toilets are on the south and north side of the parking lot. Additional outdoor toilets are located at the picnic area a half mile south of the start. There are water pumps at the shelter and picnic area. The nearby town of Plymouth (7 miles to the east) has all services, including outstanding dining and lodging at 52 Stafford, an Irish-themed inn.

Fees: A daily or annual state park pass is required to enter via car. Pay at the booth or self-pay station at the entrance to the Group Camp parking lot. The Kettle Moraine Nordic Ski Club, which grooms the trails, has a donation box at the shelter.

Events: Northern Kettle Moraine Ski Club Challenge race, fourth Sunday in January.

Phone numbers: Kettle Moraine Nordic Ski Club ski conditions hotline, (920) 467–2099; Kettle Moraine State Forest, Northern Unit, (414) 626–2116; Plymouth Chamber of Commerce, (920) 893–0079; Ice Age Park and Trail Foundation, (800) 227–0046.

The village of Greenbush has the charming appearance of a New England town. With its collection of whitewashed Greek Revival clapboard houses and churches, Greenbush is early nineteenth century America frozen in time. The town's centerpiece is the Old Wade House, once a bustling stagecoach inn on the road west from the Lake Michigan port of Sheboygan. Passed over first by the railroad and now by the highway, the days when thousands of immigrants flowed through here seeking the frontier can only be imagined.

There are no services in Greenbush. A tavern is open only sporadically. Plymouth, 7 miles to the east, is a historic small town with lots of services. This lovely community is a real gem. An Irish guest house, 52

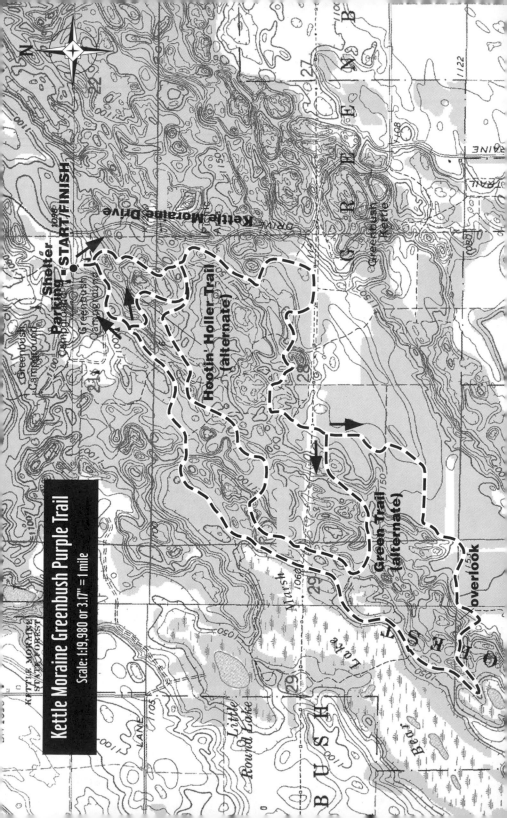

Kettle Moraine Greenbush Purple Trail

Scale: 1:19,980 or 3.17" = 1 mile

Parking = START/FINISH

Shelter

Greenbush Campground

Campground

Kettle Moraine Drive

Kettle Moraine Drive

Hootin-Holler Trail (alternate)

Green Trail (alternate)

overlook

Greenbush Kettle

KETTLE MORAINE STATE FOREST

G R E E N B U S H

Marsh

Little Round Lake

Beef

LANE

Little Round Lake

N

Stafford, is noted for its food and hospitality. A half-dozen other inns and bed and breakfasts will be found in the area.

Like the village, the trails have their own unique character. A deep, sheltering forest helps hold the snow when nearby farm fields are bare. Thanks to the dedication of the local Kettle Moraine Nordic Ski Club, the ski trails are groomed for classical skiing and skating as frequently and as well as possible. The new enclosed shelter building adds to the charm. A link of the Ice Age Trail passes by and is wonderful for snowshoeing (see page 31).

You'll agree the kettles make great skiing. The deep glacial depressions put excitement in the downhills. The trails are easy to follow in a counterclockwise direction. All are marked by periodic white posts with color-coding at the tops. Trails split off and rejoin, so multiple colors are common. If you were to ski all of the trails individually, you would cover nearly 11 miles.

The 5.1-mile Purple Trail gives a good taste of the roller-coaster ski experience without being too overwhelming. The first 0.5 mile between the trailhead shelter and the picnic area is your initiation. This wide two-way section is about as tough as it gets. Beyond the picnic area the trails are one-way. If you need an easier ski, try the Brown Trail.

The Purple Trail keeps giving you breaks from the technical kettle action. Almost immediately, there is a short, tricky, downhill left turn followed by an easy 0.25-mile cruise through a pine plantation. A

Directions at a glance

0.0 From the shelter, ski south past the trailhead sign board, going uphill on an extra-wide trail. It is color-coded with all trail colors (brown, pink, red, green, and purple).

0.1 Turn left (east) at a "T" intersection at the top of the hill.

0.5 Continue in a southerly direction at a picnic area, following purple color-coded posts (other color trails will split off of the Purple Trail as you proceed).

1.8 Continue straight (south) on the Purple Trail as the Green Trail turns right. *Alternate route:* Turn right (west) on the Green Trail. It is an advanced skier trail that totals 3.6 miles, including the portion already skied.

4.7 Continue straight (northeast) on the Purple Trail; another purple marked trail turns ninety degrees to the right and immediately begins a steep climb. *Alternate route:* Turn right (south) on the purple marked trail known as Hootin' Holler. It is a most difficult, experts-only trail that adds 0.6 mile to the Purple Trail loop.

5.0 Turn left (north) on the extra-wide all-color trail and return 0.1 mile to the shelter.

The Greenbush Purple Trail rolls through a hardwood forest.

short downhill with a left at the bottom starts another dose of great kettle skiing. Just after this turn you'll cross a snowmobile trail. Skiers have the right of way, but it's always best to use caution.

A gently rolling mile-long stretch is next. Shortly after crossing the power line the Green Trail splits off. The Green loop is the toughest in the system, with constant steep ups and downs. The easy run on the Purple Trail is followed by the most difficult downhill on the loop. Right after passing the scenic overlook bench you'll begin moderate descent into a left-hand turn, followed by a steeper slope and a tight right-hander.

Now you are in for some easy rhythm skiing for 1.25 miles along the east side of open Bear Lake Marsh. This is a nice break from the deep woods, especially when the sun is in the west. Looking uphill to the east near the end of this run, you may spot skiers taking on the tough Green Trail.

Shortly after returning into the woods for the last 0.5 mile of rolling terrain, you'll be presented with the option of taking a purple signed trail that splits off to the right. This trail bypasses the shelter link. The immediate steep uphill should tell you what's in store. It can take you on a wild run through aptly named "Hootin' Holler," a tough workout for even the best skiers. If you're not an expert, stay left and ski back to the shelter.

How to get there

From I–43 at Sheboygan, take WI 23 west for 17 miles to County Highway A. Turn south on County Highway A and follow it 0.5 mile to a stop sign in the Village of Greenbush. Go straight across Plank Road on County Highway T for 0.9 mile. Turn left (south) onto Kettle Moraine Drive, following brown-and-white Greenbush Group Camp signs for 1.3 miles; turn right (west) into the Greenbush Group Camp parking lot.

Kettle Moraine Greenbush Ice Age Trail

Greenbush, Wisconsin

Type of trail:	
Also used by:	Hikers
Distance:	2.2 miles round-trip (2.6 with Greenbush Kettle side trip)
Terrain:	Rolling
Trail difficulty:	More difficult
Surface quality:	Ungroomed, snowshoer and hiker packed
Food and facilities:	An enclosed heated shelter at the trailhead parking lot is always open. Fairly well maintained men's and women's outdoor toilets are on the south and north side of the parking lot. Additional outdoor toilets are located at the picnic area a half mile south of the start. Shelter #5, a three-sided Adirondack-type structure with a primitive outdoor toilet, is near the south end of this route. There is a hand water pump shortly before Shelter #5. Call forest headquarters for winter camping reservations.
Fees:	See "Fees" on page 27.
Phone numbers:	See "Phone numbers" on page 27.
Equipment note:	Traditional or modern snowshoes will be good for the section to Shelter #5. Modern snowshoes and at least one ski pole should be used for the side trip to the Greenbush Kettle.

Venturing onto the Ice Age Trail on snowshoes will take you on a beautiful section of the now half-completed 1,000-mile cross-state trail. The Ice Age Trail traces the features of the last continental glacier. Here it twists and rolls through the deep woods of paper birch, oak, maple, and pine. Your destination is Shelter #5 or the Greenbush Kettle. The open Adirondack-type shelter is available for winter camping by reservation.

You'll cover classic interlobate moraine. The Green Bay and Lake

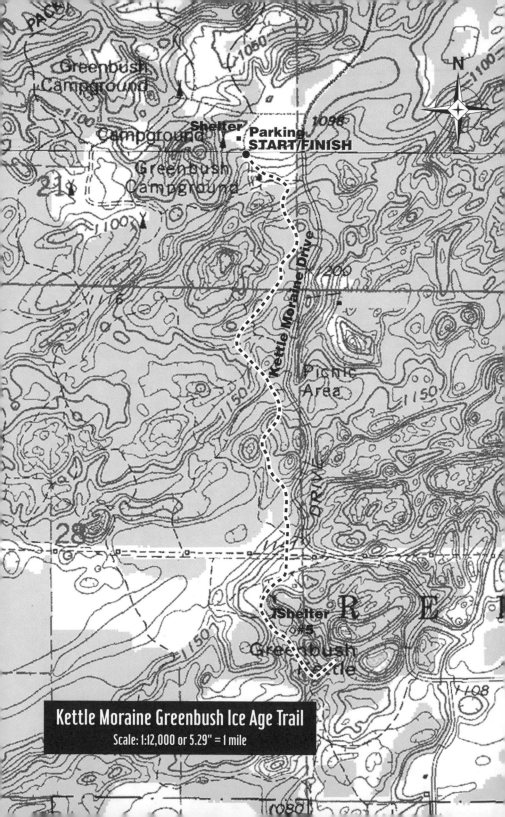

Kettle Moraine Greenbush Ice Age Trail
Scale: 1:12,000 or 5.29" = 1 mile

Michigan ice sheets of the last great glacier ground against each other here, creating the deep depressions that are the area's signature feature. The grinding ice sheets buried huge blocks of ice in the earth. When they melted they left kettles, pitlike features with no outlets, for which the forest is named.

This link of the Ice Age Trail shares the same start/finish point as the Greenbush Purple Trail.

From the Greenbush Group Camp parking area, the trail climbs up onto a steep ridge between the ski trail and Kettle Moraine Drive. Through the trees you may see skiers gliding along on the west side and/or to the east, spot an occasional car on the road. As you approach the picnic area the trail dips and twists before climbing into the open.

Continuing south from the picnic area, you plunge down into the woods and weave between three deep kettles. Leaving the kettles, the trail climbs over a steep ridge and crosses a power line as it emerges from the woods. Following an old road, the trail swings west then south as it re-enters the forest just before it reaches Shelter #5, located off-trail to the left.

If you choose to take the side trip to the Greenbush Kettle, you are in

Directions at a glance

0.0   From the shelter, skirt the south edge of the parking lot and head southeast past the men's toilet and uphill across an open field.

0.05 Turn right (southwest) on the Ice Age Trail, following yellow color-coded posts and yellow-and-white painted tree blazes.

0.6   Turn right (south) on the ski trail and follow it between the picnic area toilet buildings. Continue straight (south) and look for the resumption of the Ice Age Trail just to the left of the ski trail.

1.1   Turn around at the open shelter (#5) 30 yards off the trail to the left and return to the start.

Side trip

1.1   Continue south on the Ice Age Trail for a view of the Greenbush Kettle.

1.25 Turn left (north) off of the Ice Age Trail at the very top of a steep climb immediately after a yellow-and-white blazed tree on the left. Follow the ridge line trail down for 250 feet for a good view of Greenbush Kettle.

1.3   Turn around and return to the start of the Ice Age Trail.

for a very steep climb. The trail enters a notch in the moraine and the only way out is up. On top a short side trail will take you along the ridge line to a fine overview of the deep, symmetrical shape of Greenbush Kettle.

How to get there
See "How to get there" on page 31.

When monstrous buried blocks of ice melted they created "kettle" pits.

Ledge View Nature Center Ledge Walk Trail

Chilton, Wisconsin

Type of trail: ▬ ≤ ⬤

Distance: 1.2 miles (1.3 miles with snowshoe only option)

Terrain: Flat to rolling (steeper sections on snowshoe-only option)

Trail difficulty: Easy

Surface quality: Groomed and double tracked except on snowshoe trails

Food and facilities: Parking, indoor heated shelter, soda vending machine, hot chocolate and indoor toilets are at the trailhead. All services are available in Chilton, including primo microbrewed beers (if you like darks try Total Eclipse) at Rowland's Calumet Brewing Co. and home cooking at Marcal's Restaurant.

Events: Guided snowshoe hikes, Sundays in January and February; evening Cross-country Ski, Saturday nearest the full moon in January.

Phone numbers: Ledge View Nature Center, (920) 849–7094; Chilton Chamber of Commerce, (920) 849–4540.

Ledge View Nature Center occupies the high ground 150 feet above the gently rolling farmland of eastern Wisconsin. That doesn't mean you'll have to tackle severe terrain to ski or snowshoe here. The trail is mostly on the flat hilltop. The greatest elevation change, even on the snowshoe-only option, will be 40 feet and that will be gentle. The comfortable, modern Nature Center is a wonderful facility that features exhibits on flora and fauna. There are three caves at Ledge View that penetrate the Niagara dolomite capstone. They can be toured in the summer.

Your big decision may be whether to ski or snowshoe. Either is easy. Once you're there you'll know Ledge View is a snowshoe place. Inside the Nature Center there are dozens and dozens of snowshoes to rent. Outside, snowshoe tracks go everywhere; it isn't unusual to see whole busloads of area schoolchildren traipsing around on them. When I visited, an

Kids sprint in an impromptu snowshoe race at Ledge View Nature Center.

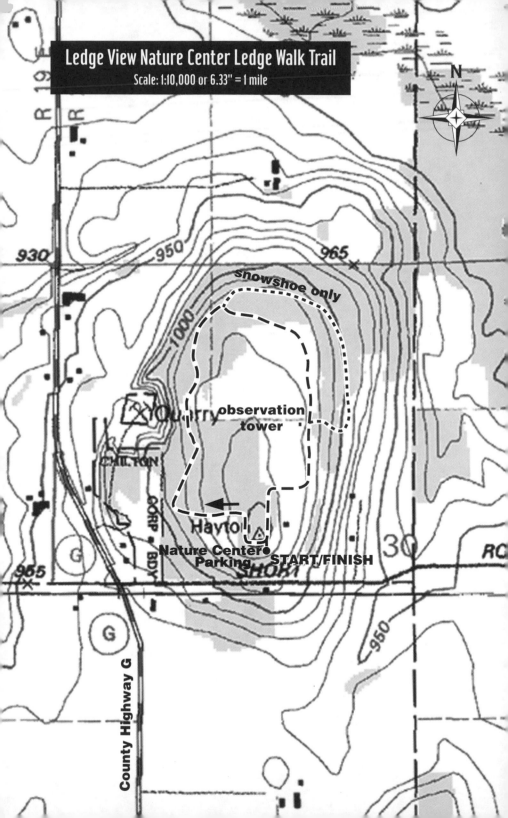

impromptu snowshoe race was staged for enthusiastic kids at the end of their tour.

The hilltop is a contrast of hardwood forest and open prairie. Leaving the Nature Center the Ledge View Trail soon heads into the aspen, paper birch, and sugar maple woods. The maples are tapped for their sweet sap in March and boiled down for syrup.

Maple syrup and sugar are two of the many Native American gifts we all enjoy. The Ojibwe made sugar all March, then lived on it almost exclusively in April. It fueled tremendous feats like hauling huge loads of fur pelts and supplies to the Lake Michigan shore and canoeing hundreds of miles to rendezvous with traders. The Ojibwe now celebrate spring by making maple syrup snow cones for their children.

The trail gradually descends to its westernmost point before turning north, making an even more gradual climb through the woods. Following the hill's contour lines the trail twists and turns over gently rolling ground as it heads north. If you are on snowshoes, follow the route of the ski trail. You'll notice that snowshoe tracks go everywhere in the woods. You could easily get turned around off the trail.

At the northern point of the ski-tracked loop, snowshoers can head downhill and follow an ungroomed loop around to the observation tower. This segment will be more wooded than the ski trail.

When you reach the tower, take time to climb to the top if it isn't icy. The view from the top is wonderful. A maple syrup snow cone would make it perfect.

Directions at a glance

0.0 From the northeast side of the Nature Center building, go north on the groomed double track trail or, if snowshoeing, follow the trail off to the side. Turn left (west) 20 yards from the start. YOU ARE HERE map signs are at many intersections.

0.2 Continue straight (west) as the Ledge Walk Trail merges on the left. You are now on the Ledge View Trail, which immediately turns to the north.

0.6 Continue straight (southeast) on skis or turn left (north) on snowshoes to follow the Ledge Walk Trail, adding on 0.1 mile to the trip.

0.9 (1.0 on snowshoes) Continue straight (south) on skis or turn left (south) on snowshoes at the observation tower. Follow to trailhead.

How to get there

From U.S. 151 in Chilton, go 1 mile south on County Highway G. Turn east on Short Road for 0.2 mile and turn north into the Ledge View Nature Center drive.

Calumet Park Effigy Mounds Trail
Hilbert, Wisconsin

Type of trail: ▬▬▬

Distance: 1.7 miles

Terrain: Mostly flat with several steep sections

Trail difficulty: More difficult

Surface quality: Groomed, double tracked

Food and facilities: Parking is at the park office trailhead. Indoor shelter, beverages, snacks, and toilets are at the park office and Coffee Tree Lodge on weekends and daily during the Christmas holiday period except December 24 and 25. Fish Tails supper club, near the park entrance, serves lunch and dinner Tuesday through Sunday. Some services are available in Sherwood, 7 miles north. All services are available in the Fox Cities (Appleton, Kimberly, Little Chute, and Kaukauna) 15 miles northwest, including ski retail and repair.

Phone numbers: Calumet County Parks Department, (920) 439–1008; Fox Cities Convention and Visitors Bureau, (920) 734–3356.

Lake Winnebago can be a beautiful and foreboding place in winter. The view of the huge inland lake from Calumet Park is little changed since Native Americans built panther-shaped ceremonial mounds on the bluff top. Over the bluff a wonderful system of ski trails winds in and out of the woods. At the north end an old slope serves as a tubing run.

Directions at a glance

0.0   From the back side of the park office, go south on the groomed trail, following Nature Trail signs.

0.1   Turn left (east) at a "T" intersection then immediately right (south).

0.6   Continue straight (south) at a four-way intersection, following the trail signed UPPER PARK as the trail signed LAKE SHORE turns right.

0.9   Cross the park road and turn left (north) through the fence line as the other trail goes straight.

1.4   Bear left (northwest), cross the park road, and follow the orange-and-black CAUTION sign to a long downhill run.

1.6   Turn left (southwest) at the Coffee Tree Lodge and continue to trailhead.

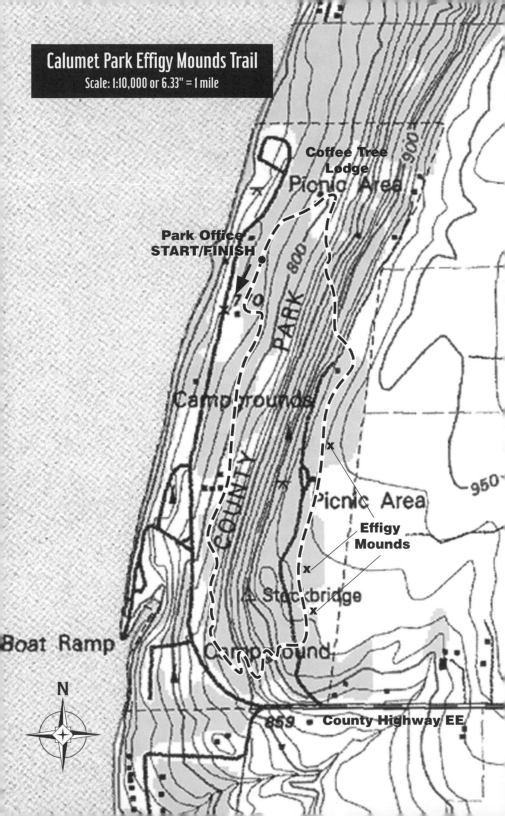

Calumet Park Effigy Mounds Trail
Scale: 1:10,000 or 6.33" = 1 mile

Coffee Tree Lodge

Picnic Area

Park Office
START/FINISH

PARK 800

Campgrounds

COUNTY

Picnic Area

Effigy
Mounds

Stockbridge

Boat Ramp

N

Campground

859   County Highway EE

900

950

Snowplowing is the way to handle the 170-foot drop at Calumet County Park.

The bluff is the edge of the Niagara Escarpment, a tough layer of limestone that forms the east shore of the lake and stretches all the way to Niagara Falls. Its 170-foot height might earn this counterclockwise loop a most difficult rating if it weren't for the six switchback turns that lessen the grade on the climb, and the straight, smooth, evenly graded downhill run. Still, it is at the upper end of the more difficult rating; the ability to control speed by snowplowing is essential.

The mostly one-way trail system isn't particularly well marked, but because the trails are in such a compact area, it really doesn't matter. On the lower level, the Effigy Mounds Trail winds through a beautiful stand of cedars. These give way to maples as you herringbone the switchbacks up to the top. Once there, you ski through open areas past the park's four panther mounds.

Panther profiles were only one of the animal shapes this mysterious Native American culture created over nearly a thousand years. Effigy mound building ended hundreds of years before European contact. Bears, swallows, turtles, buffalo, lizards, eagles, deer, and even human shapes were made. They sometimes contained human remains, sometimes dogs, often nothing.

The mystery of the mounds comes from the lack of grave items or any association with village sites. They were almost always built near lakes, marshes, or rivers. Just recently, about 40 miles south of here, low stones were found among a mound group. On solstice and equinox sunsets, the stones and mounds align; one arrangement of stones had the same form as the constellation Scorpio—a Wisconsin Stonehenge.

Leaving the mounds behind, the trail heads back into a wooded campground area. The campsites are unused in winter. The trail crosses the unplowed park road where an orange CAUTION sign alerts you to the long, steep, 120-foot downhill run that takes you to the base of the old downhill area. Swinging southwest past the Coffee Tree Lodge, another 40 feet of elevation are lost on the short run to the park office/trailhead.

How to get there
From Sherwood, go south on WI 55 for 5.5 miles and turn right on County Highway EE. Go 1.2 miles to the Calumet County Park entrance road and follow it to the park office.

Point Beach State Forest Rawley Point Trail
Two Rivers, Wisconsin

Type of trail:	🎿
Also used by:	Hikers
Distance:	1.8 miles round-trip
Terrain:	Flat to rolling
Trail difficulty:	Easy
Surface quality:	Ungroomed
Food and facilities:	A porta-type outdoor toilet is near the Rawley Point Lighthouse historical marker. All services are available in Two Rivers, 5 miles south. Manitowoc, twelve miles south, and Two Rivers are great places for food. With their lake heritage, fish is always on the menu. Check out Kristina's Gourmet Cafe in Manitowoc or the Water's Edge Restaurant at the Lighthouse Inn in Two Rivers.
Fees:	A daily or annual parking pass is required to enter via car. Pay at the entrance booth or self-pay station.
Phone numbers:	Manitowoc–Two Rivers Area Chamber of Commerce, (800) 262–7892 or (414) 684–5575.

There is nothing more foreboding than the rolling blue-gray waves of Lake Michigan on a winter day. Wear windproof pants and a windbreaker and be glad you don't live the life of the men who once sailed wooden ships on her waters.

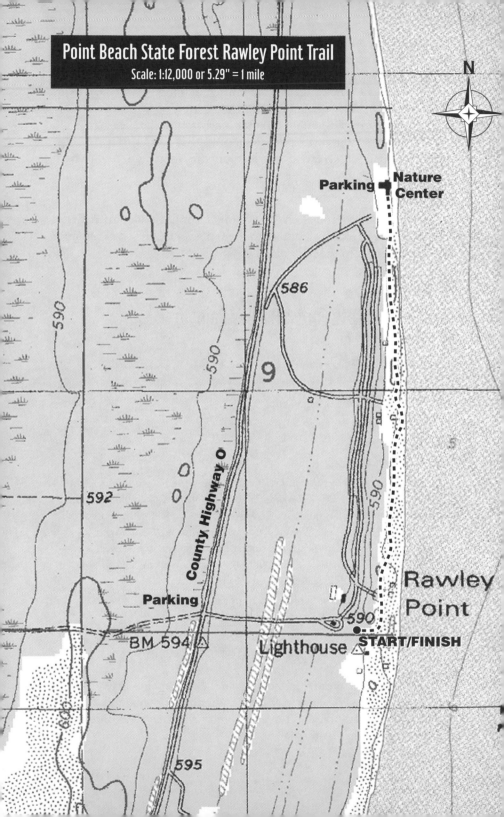

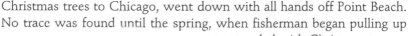

For a century-and-a-half, Rawley Point Lighthouse has been a beacon for sailors on treacherous Lake Michigan.

The picturesque, 113-foot-tall Rawley Point Lighthouse tells part of the story. There has been a light on this point since 1853. It was in the mid–nineteenth century that steps were taken to make shipping safer on the treacherous lake. Ships sailed north and south; storms blew from the east or west, driving the ships onto points like this.

Despite the danger, wooden sailing ships kept hauling goods on Lake Michigan well into the twentieth Century. Wooden ships were cheap and sailors expendable. In a November storm in 1912 the *Rouse Simmons*, a three-masted schooner carrying Christmas trees to Chicago, went down with all hands off Point Beach. No trace was found until the spring, when fisherman began pulling up nets tangled with Christmas trees.

The Manitowoc Maritime Museum, 11 miles south, has excellent exhibits on shipbuilding on the lake. They don't dwell on the tragedies, but rather focus on design and craftsmanship. You can also tour the USS *Cobia,* a WWII submarine, one of twenty-eight built at a local shipyards.

There isn't much of a trail here. It's pretty distinct when you start out; after the picnic area it's best to go out to the dunes and find your own way north. The dunes are also a good spot for a photo of the lighthouse and crashing lake waves.

Directions at a glance

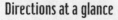

0.0 From the Rawley Point Lighthouse historical marker, go east on the trail that passes just left of the marker. Forty yards farther the trail bends to the north.

0.15 Bear right at the Rawley Point Picnic Area and continue north among the dunes. There is no marked trail from here on.

0.9 Turn around at the Nature Center and return to the trailhead.

How to get there

From WI 42 in Two Rivers, go east then north on County Highway O for 5 miles. Turn right (east) at the Point Beach State Forest Campground sign. Go 0.2 mile and park at the Rawley Point Lighthouse historical marker.

Point Beach State Forest Red Pine Trail

Two Rivers, Wisconsin

Type of trail:	━━━
Distance:	3.4 miles
Terrain:	Flat to rolling
Trail difficulty:	Easy
Surface quality:	Groomed periodically, double tracked
Food and facilities:	A porta-type outdoor toilet is near the Rawley Point Lighthouse historical marker. All services are available in Two Rivers, 5 miles south. Manitowoc, 12 miles south, and Two Rivers are great places for food. With their lake heritage, fish is always on the menu. Check out Kristina's Gourmet Cafe in Manitowoc or the Water's Edge Restaurant at the Lighthouse Inn in Two Rivers.
Fees:	A daily or annual parking pass is required to enter via car. Pay at the entrance booth or self-pay station.
Phone numbers:	Manitowoc–Two Rivers Area Chamber of Commerce, (800) 262–7892 or (414) 684–5575.

Where do old sand dunes go? Inland is the answer. They are replaced by new dunes. Gradually, grass and trees take hold on the old slopes. As the years pass, there is little to show they were ever dunes except for telltale ridges that run parallel to the beach.

Directions at a glance

0.0   From the west side of the Nature Center parking lot, go west on the two-way groomed trail signed SKI, HIKING & NATURE TRAIL, SWALES NATURE TRAIL. The ungroomed Swales trail splits off to the right after a short distance. Follow the blue-and-white skier silhouette signs.

0.3   Cross County Highway O.

0.4   Turn right (north) on the one-way ski trail.

2.4   Turn left (north) at a four-way intersection. The south end parking lot is to the right.

3.0   Turn right (east) on the two-way trail.

3.1   Cross County Highway O and follow the trail to the trailhead.

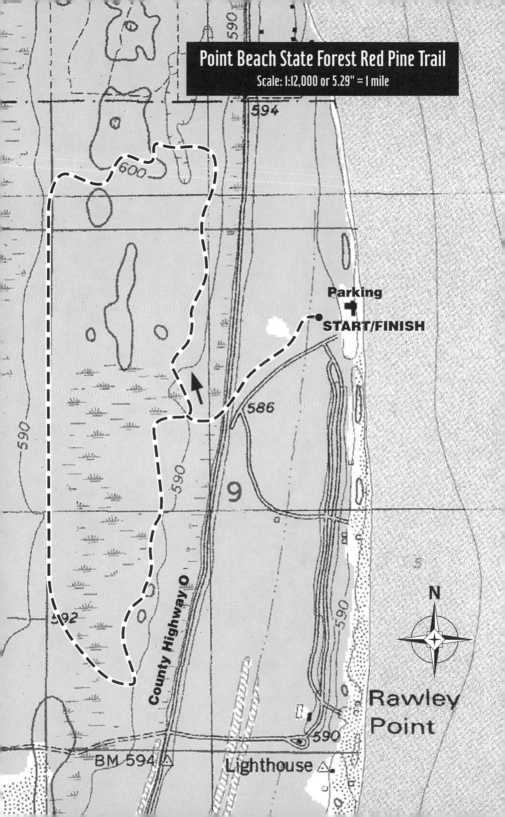

Point Beach State Forest Red Pine Trail
Scale: 1:12,000 or 5.29" = 1 mile

594

600

Parking
START/FINISH

586

590

9

590

592

County Highway O

N

Rawley
Point

590

BM 594

590

Lighthouse

You'll ski over old wooded dunes on the Red Pine Trail. Starting at the Nature Center (too bad nothing is open in winter) you go west on a flat two-way trail across County Highway O. A right turn puts you on the one-way counterclockwise loop. Periodic YOU ARE HERE map signs give confidence. Soon you are up on a dune ridge, gliding north through a beautiful stand of birch and hemlock.

Swinging around to the west, the trail begins to snake around and you come to the only challenging turns, two right-handers anyone can handle by snowplowing. Nothing is more than 25 feet in elevation. A turn to the south puts you on a straight, flat, mile-long stretch through stands of red pine. A sharp left at a four-way intersection brings on more rolling terrain before you head back to the beach.

How to get there

From WI 42 in Two Rivers, go east then north on County Highway O for 5 miles. Turn right (east) at the Point Beach State Forest Campground sign. Go east then north on the park road for 1 mile to the Nature Center parking lot. The trailhead is across the lot from the Nature Center.

Easy striding on hemlock- and birch-lined ridge trails.

Blue Mound State Park Indian Marker Tree Trail

Blue Mounds, Wisconsin

Type of trail:	⬭
Also used by:	Hikers
Distance:	1.3 miles
Terrain:	Rolling, with very steep sections
Trail difficulty:	More difficult
Surface quality:	Ungroomed, hiker and snowshoer packed
Food and facilities:	Parking for the start/finish is on the road to the West Observation Tower (the lot is usually unplowed). There is a plowed parking lot at the East Observation Tower. Outdoor toilets are near each tower. Porta-type toilets are at the ski trailhead near the swimming pool. The park also has cross-country ski trails (see page 51). There are taverns in the town of Blue Mounds, 2 miles southeast. Winter campsites are available in the state park. All services are available in Mount Horeb, 7 miles east, including home cooking at Schubert's Cafe and Bakery on Main Street (County Highway ID), where you can get the best macaroons imaginable. Mount Horeb also has a new brewpub/restaurant.
Fees:	A daily or annual state park pass is required to enter via car. Pay at the entrance booth or self-pay station.
Phone numbers:	Mount Horeb Area Chamber of Commerce, (608) 437–5914; Blue Mound State Park, (608) 437–5711.
Equipment note:	Modern or bear paw traditional snowshoes with ski poles will be best.

With the relentless building and paving of modern society, it is amazing to think you might still find reminders of the centuries when Native Americans traveled this land. Blue Mound, the highest point in southern Wisconsin, was a sacred place to them. They called the haze, which often hangs over the top, smoke of the Great Spirit. For thousands of years they came here to gather chert, a cream-colored flintlike rock used to make cutting tools and spear and arrow points. The trail you snowshoe follows their ancient path.

As you descend from the mound top, you soon come to a marker tree. Native Americans bent young trees to indicate direction of travel, and the trees would continue to grow in that shape. The one on the trail is believed to have been planted around 1860, more than a hundred years after the introduction of European trade goods. Because there was no

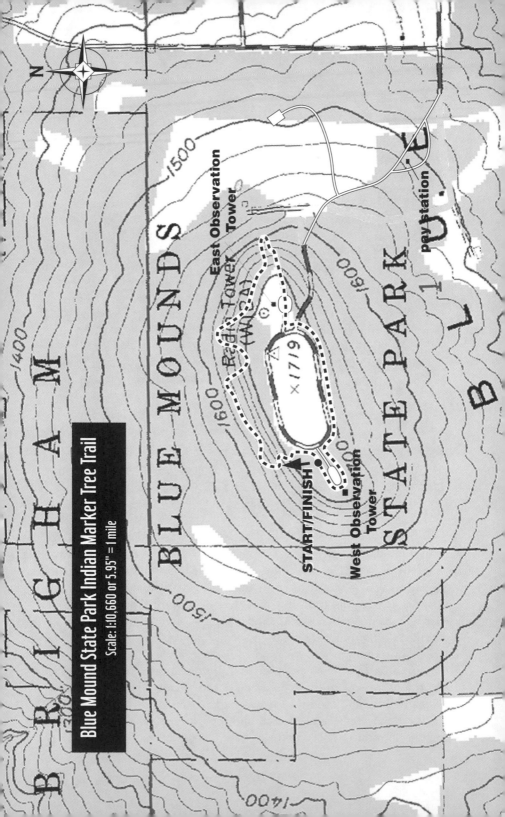

N

Blue Mound State Park Indian Marker Tree Trail
Scale: 1:10,660 or 5.95" = 1 mile

BRIGHAM

BLUE MOUNDS

BLUE MOUNDS STATE PARK

BLUE

1500

1400

1300

1400

1500

1500

1600

1600

1600

1700

×1719

1700

1600

1500

1400

East Observation Tower

Radio Tower (W124)

START/FINISH

West Observation Tower

pay station

Directions at a glance

0.0   From the north side of the West Observation Tower road, snow-shoe east along the road then north along the loop road.

0.05 Turn left (northwest) onto the Indian Marker Tree Trail (brown-and-white sign) and begin descending.

0.1   Turn right (east) shortly after the Indian Marker Tree. The trail is hardly marked at all from here on. If no one else has hiked or snowshoed it (likely) you will have to rely on your trail-finding skills. The trail roughly parallels the contour of Blue Mound. You will not climb or descend for any great distance and the uphill will always be on your right.

0.4   Continue straight (east) at a crossing of the Flint Rock Trail.

0.7   Make a radical, nearly 180 degree turn (west) as you enter an open area and see a sign indicating that the Spring House is straight ahead. Once around the turn you will see a sign: PICNIC AREA .1 MILE. Begin climbing steeply.

0.8   Continue west at the East Observation Tower.

0.9   Turn left (south) and cross the paved park entrance road. Follow the south side of the loop road.

1.25 Loop around the West Observation Tower parking lot (northeast) and return to start/finish.

longer a need for chert, they must have continued to climb Blue Mound for spiritual reasons.

The trail has many twists and turns. It may be a bit hard to follow if it hasn't been hiked or snowshoed. The path is narrow and at times difficult to distinguish from other openings in the trees. Think of this as a chance to test your trail-finding skills. You will roughly follow the mound's contour lines around, so don't go up or down too far and always keep the uphill side on your right. You can nearly always see the top of the mound. The East Observation Tower can be spotted through the trees long before getting to it.

The toughest part of the route comes after making a near 180 degree turn toward the tower. You'll climb more than 100 feet in just over 100 yards. The observation towers are not maintained for winter use, but they are often free of snow and ice due to exposure to wind and sun. The views from the towers are wonderful and well worth the climb. Hold onto your hat if it's windy.

How to get there

From U.S. 18/151, 3 miles west of Mount Horeb, turn north on County Highway F, following brown-and-white signs to Blue Mound State Park. At a "T" intersection after 0.3 mile turn left (west) on County Highway ID. At 0.8 mile turn right (north) onto Mounds Road into the town of Blue Mounds and follow it to the park entrance. Follow the park road for 1 mile to the parking area for the west observation tower.

The 140-year-old marker tree still points the way at Blue Mound.

Blue Mound State Park Willow Springs Trail

Blue Mounds, Wisconsin

Type of trail:	
Distance:	1.9 miles
Terrain:	Rolling, with some long, steep sections
Trail difficulty:	More difficult
Surface quality:	Groomed, single tracked, skate lane
Food and facilities:	See "Food and facilities" on page 47.
Fees:	A daily or annual state park pass is required to enter via car. Pay at the entrance booth or self-pay station.
Phone numbers:	Mount Horeb Area Chamber of Commerce, (608) 437–5914; Blue Mound State Park, (608) 437–5711.

There is something nice about a ski trail that starts out running downhill. Especially when it's gradual enough for an exhilarating warm-up, which is needed to handle the long 180-foot climb on the backside. Willow Springs loop is just such a perfect trail.

Blue Mound owes its preeminence as one of the state's highest spots to a capstone of Niagara dolomite, the same layer of rock Niagara Falls tumbles over. All other remnants of the sedimentary limestone eroded all the way back to eastern Wisconsin. This gift of nature has left a cone-shaped hill and a wonderful place to ski.

Leaving the swimming pool trailhead, you'll drop 100 feet in 0.3 mile as you follow the trail in a counterclockwise direction. Then a 90 degree turn to the northwest will take you on a gently rolling stretch for 0.25 mile. Even then the climb comes on gradually. After another 0.25 mile, the skiing gets tough in a hurry. You will climb 100 feet in 0.1 mile before the grade lessens. Fortunately, the last 0.25 mile is also a gradual downhill.

The circuit is almost entirely in the

A dense fog frosts the trees high up on Blue Mound.

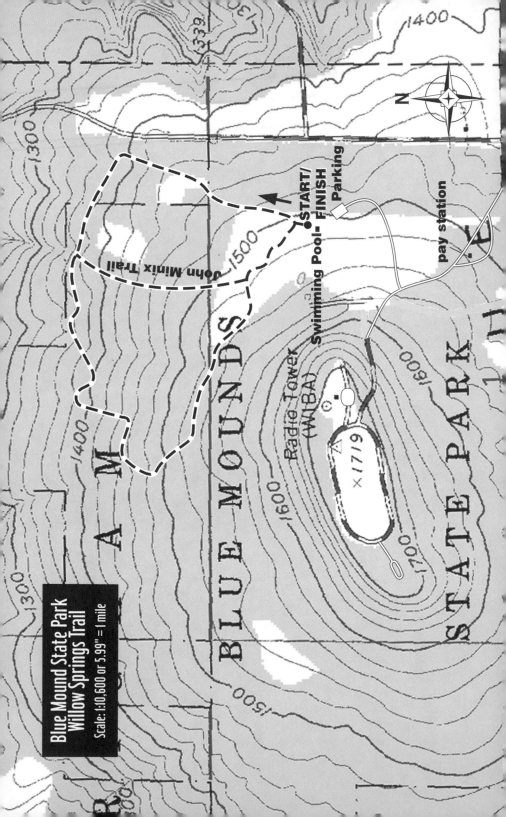

Blue Mound State Park
Willow Springs Trail
Scale: 1:10,600 or 5.99" = 1 mile

START/FINISH

Parking

Swimming Pool

pay station

John Minix Trail

Radio Tower (WIBA)

× 1719

BLUE MOUNDS STATE PARK

N

1400

1300

1500

1600

1700

deep hardwood forest that covers the mound's slopes. This makes a nice refuge on a windy day, which might be bitter in an open area. The adjacent 2-mile-long Pleasant Valley Loop is just such an open trail. The woods also keep the snow nicer longer. Good snow is something the park is often blessed with thanks to its higher elevation. If you are up for a long ski you can circle the entire mound by combining these trails with the Flint Rock and Ridgeview for a total distance of 5 miles.

How to get there

From U.S. 18/151, 3 miles west of Mount Horeb, turn north on County Highway F, following brown-and-white signs to Blue Mound State Park. At a "T" intersection, after 0.3 mile, turn left (west) on County Highway ID. At 0.8 mile turn right (north) onto Mounds Road into the town of Blue Mounds and follow it to the park entrance. Follow the park road for 0.4 mile to the entrance of the swimming pool area on the right. Follow it past the pool to the far end of the parking area.

Directions at a glance

0.0 From the trailhead sign board at the north end of the swimming pool parking area, head north on the groomed two-way trail, following blue-and-white skier silhouette signs.

0.05 Turn right (east) as a trail marked DO NOT ENTER merges from the left.

0.1 Continue straight (north) as the Pleasure Valley Loop splits off to the right. You are now on the combined one-way John Minix, Willow Springs, and Flint Rock Loops. YOU ARE HERE signs are at most intersections.

0.7 Continue straight (west) as the John Minix Loop turns off to the left.

1.1 Turn left (southeast) as the Flint Rock Loop turns right.

1.7 Continue straight (east) as the John Minix Loop merges from the left.

1.85 Turn right (south) and follow the short two-way spur back to the trailhead.

The Springs Winter Wonder Land Trail
Spring Green, Wisconsin

Type of trail: ▬ ◄

Distance: 1.8 miles

Terrain: Flat to rolling

Trail difficulty: Easy

Surface quality: Groomed, single tracked, skate lane

Food and facilities: Parking, indoor heated shelter and toilets, food and drink, lodging, and ski rentals are available at the trailhead. Spring Green has interesting galleries, lodging, and restaurants in town or in the area. You can find more affordable Taliesin Fellowship–designed lodging nearby at the Usonian Inn or the Spring Valley Inn. The latter is also a good place to enjoy a meal or a microbrew. The Round Barn in Spring Green is a landmark inn and restaurant. For a light lunch try the General Store/Spring Green Cafe. Friday night fish fries at the Post House Restaurant are terrific.

Phone numbers: The Springs, (608) 588–7000; Spring Green Chamber of Commerce, (608) 588–2042 or (800) 588–2042.

In a way, The Springs resort is the fulfillment of one of Frank Lloyd Wright's dreams. Wright, who built his home and architecture school, Taliesin and Taliesin Fellowship, in the neighboring valley, envisioned a recreational complex featuring many types of sports. He was the world's most productive designer, but even though he lived to 90, finances kept him from realizing the project. The nearby Frank Lloyd Wright Visitor Center, originally a restaurant, was the only structure built.

The Springs was designed by the Taliesin Fellowship, which carries on Wright's architectural tradition. It overlooks the valley and bluffs that inspired Wright to create designs that harmonized with nature. Lodging and dining at the Springs are top-notch. This is no rustic ski weekend experience. There is a spa, indoor pool, whirlpool, therapeutic massage,

Directions at a glance

0.0 From the golf pro shop, ski south on the two-way groomed Winter Wonder Land Trail.

0.05 Turn left to ski the loop clockwise.

0.9 Continue straight (west) as the Blackhawk Trail turns left.

1.6 Turn right (northwest) as the Birch Ridge Loop turns left.

1.75 Turn left and return to trailhead.

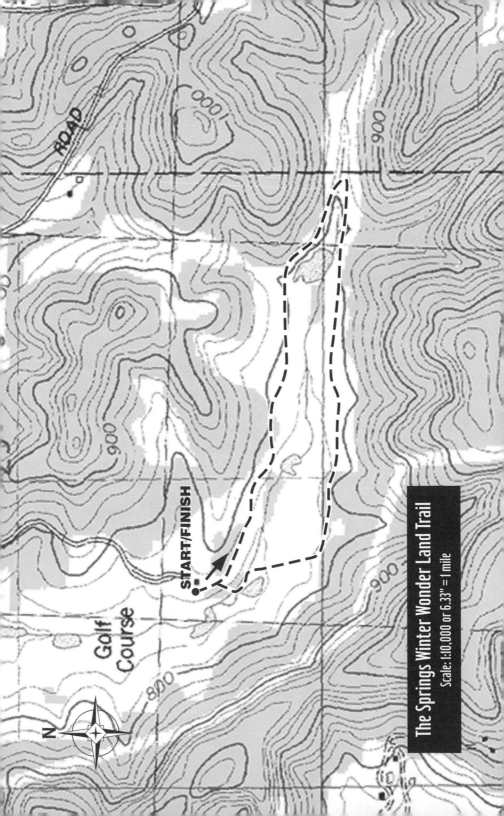

ROAD

900

900

900

900

START/FINISH

Golf Course

800

N

The Springs Winter Wonder Land Trail
Scale: 1:10,000 or 6.33" = 1 mile

The dining room at The Springs looks out on the ski trails and wooded bluffs.

even a workout room. If you ski, you won't need the workout room, but you might need the whirlpool or massage.

The Winter Wonder Land loop shouldn't be too hard on you. It is really the easiest way to enjoy the wonderful valley scenery on skis. Other easy loops follow similar gently rolling terrain to the north. Advanced or expert skiers may want to take on the ridge trails. All are accessed from the Blackhawk Trail, which turns south off of Winter Wonder Land and up the 250-foot bluffs. In all, there are another 12 miles of ski trails here.

Skiing clockwise from the golf pro shop, Winter Wonder Land reveals the beauty of the oak-forested bluff sides. The bluffs close in as you ski toward the turnaround. The narrowing valley is a perfect example of a landform untouched by the leveling hand of the continental glacier. It inspires people today as it once inspired Frank Lloyd Wright.

How to get there

From U.S. 14 at Spring Green, go south on WI 23 for 3 miles. Turn left (east) on County Highway C, go 0.6 mile and turn right (south) on Tower Road. Go 0.3 mile and turn right on The Springs entrance road. Follow to the resort and park near the golf pro shop on the north end.

Devils Lake State Park Ice Age Trail

Baraboo, Wisconsin

Type of trail:	▬ ◄
Distance:	7.1 miles
Terrain:	Rolling and hilly with very steep sections
Trail difficulty:	Most difficult
Surface quality:	Groomed periodically, single tracked, skate lane
Food and facilities:	Parking at the lower trailhead. A porta-type outdoor toilet is at the Steinke Basin trailhead. All services are available in Baraboo, 3 miles north, including the excellent Little Village Cafe.
Fees:	A daily or annual state park pass is required to enter via car. Pay at the park headquarters on the way in.
Phone numbers:	Baraboo Area Chamber of Commerce, (800) 227–2266; Devils Lake State Park, (608) 356–8301.

Devils Lake State Park is one of Wisconsin's most popular summer destinations. In winter it pretty much shuts down. The beachside concession building is closed; there isn't even a shelter. So why is this trail in the book? One big reason: a mile-plus downhill run. You won't find that anywhere else in the state.

The long downhill isn't the only motivation for visiting in winter. Devils Lake is incredibly beautiful and perhaps the most geologically significant place in the state. It seems a shame that more isn't done to make winter recreation hospitable. At the same time, the solitude is soothing. The start/finish is at the north end beach, where you look south into the lake-filled gap cut through 400-foot-high quartzite bluffs. Snowmobiles are not allowed on the lake. It's quiet.

A river once ran through the gap, cutting through the 1.7-billion-year-old quartzite. A mere 16,000 years ago, the continental glacier had its last gasp here, making one last push that plugged up both ends. Scientists from around the world come to see this unique phenomenon. You'll just be spellbound by the beauty.

When I mentioned skiing downhill for a mile, any wary skier would conclude that meant one must also ski uphill for a mile. That would be correct. The climb begins immediately; the blessing is that only 260 feet are gained. Other than four very steep short sections you will herringbone, the climb is fairly gradual.

The trails are two-way. I recommend skiing the loop clockwise. On the right, as you near the top, the bluff falls away sharply. This is the side of the canyon you'll ski down later.

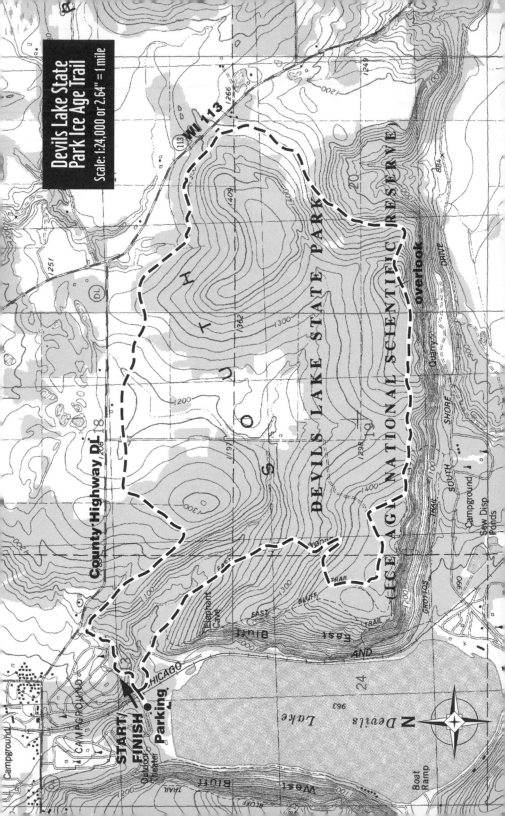

Directions at a glance

0.0   From the parking lot, ski northeast along the park road. You will follow yellow and/or red marking squares. YOU ARE HERE signs are at most intersections.

0.05 Continue straight (northeast) after crossing railroad tracks. Ski around the right side of a steel gate and onto the groomed trail with yellow and white squares and blue-and-white skier silhouettes on the Northern Lights Campground and Ice Age Campground road.

0.2   Turn right (east) off of the road onto a groomed trail through the woods just past the brown-and-white QUIET ZONE sign.

0.45 Turn right (southeast) just past the amphitheater.

1.2   Continue straight (northeast) as the East Bluff Trail splits off to the right. The intersection sign indicates you are on the Steinke and Ice Age Trails.

1.5   Continue straight (east) at the Steinke Basin trailhead onto the Ice Age Trail, following red and yellow squares.

1.8   Continue straight (east) as the Steinke Trail turns right. Follow the Ice Age Trail marked with red squares.

4.8   Continue straight (west) on the East Bluff Woods Trail marked with yellow squares as the Ice Age Trail turns right.

5.2   Turn left (west) at a "T" intersection with a black-on-orange arrow.

5.5   Turn right (north) on a trail marked with yellow squares. The orange sign for the trail straight ahead says EAST BLUFF TRAIL.

5.9   The trail curves sharply left and makes a very steep drop. Follow to trailhead.

Most of the trail is in a deep hardwood and pine forest. Once on top, it breaks out into an open area before rolling along back into the woods. Swinging around to the west, a long, steep 200-foot climb brings you to an overlook of the gap. Looking down and west you can see the plug of glacial moraine that captured the lake. There follows a 100-foot run after a 140-foot climb.

The trail lazes along on the bluff top for about 0.5 mile. A number of orange signs on side trails to the left lead to places like Devils Doorway, Moldy Buttress, and Hawk's Nest. Don't take the chance of visiting these spots on skis.

You'll know when the trail nears the 400-foot, mile-long downhill.

Yellow diamond caution signs say CAUTION, STEEP HILL, and CURVE AHEAD. They aren't kidding. The initial drop is 100 feet in about 500 feet of distance. Then the trail just snakes the rest of the way. If the snow is thin, the water bars and humps over culverts make things very exciting.

Don't ski this trail in anything other than ideal conditions. You may ski around on the bluff top trails, but don't tackle the downhill. I still remember the Swiss Army knife–shaped bruise I ended up with on my backside from trying it. No matter what the conditions, your quads will be throbbing as you break into the open at the bottom.

How to get there

Exit south from I–90/94 at the U.S. 12, Baraboo/Wisconsin Dells exit 92. Follow U.S. 12 for 9 miles; turn left (east) onto WI 159 for 1.5 miles. Turn right (south) at the "T" intersection with WI 123 and follow it 0.5 mile to the junction with County Highway DL. Go straight across County Highway DL onto the park entrance road and follow it past the park headquarters to the plowed parking lot on the right.

A snow angel on Devils Lake.

Parfrey's Glen Scientific Area Trail
Merrimac, Wisconsin

Type of trail: 🔲

Also used by: Hikers

Distance: 1.8 miles round-trip

Terrain: Flat with a few steep sections

Trail difficulty: Easy, some difficult sections at the very end

Surface quality: Ungroomed, hiker and snowshoer packed

Food and facilities: Parking may be available in the trailhead parking lot if it is plowed. Otherwise park as well as you can on the entrance road without blocking the steel gate. A water pump and outdoor toilets are at the north end of the unplowed access road. On weekends the Old Schoolhouse Restaurant, 0.25 mile east on County Highway DL, has a good, family-style all-you-can-eat breakfast. Devils Head Lodge alpine ski area, 0.25 mile north, has lodging and two restaurants. The Cornucopia is upscale; Dante's is more basic American food, cafeteria style. They tend to be crowded on ski weekends. All services are available in Baraboo, 3 miles north, including the excellent Little Village Cafe.

Fees: A daily or annual state park pass is required to park. There is a self-pay station at the trailhead.

Phone numbers: Baraboo Area Chamber of Commerce, (800) 227–2266; Devils Lake State Park, (608) 356–8301.

Equipment note: Use modern snowshoes with one ski pole if you want to go all the way to the end. Otherwise, any type of snowshoe will be fine.

Parfrey's Glen is one of the loveliest, most intimate little spots in Wisconsin. Though the inner gorge is only about 0.25-mile long, it holds enough fascination to permanently etch itself in your memory. This trek will take you deeper and deeper into an ever narrowing gorge, where each twist and turn reveal another beautiful scene.

The glen was once a place only a few people knew about by word of mouth. The 0.5-mile hike from the parking area helps keep the crowds down, but your best chance for the old experience of unfolding wonder is to visit in winter.

As you travel through the gorge, you may see reedlike segmented plants pushing up through the snow. This is scouring rush, an ancient type that predates leafy, flowering plants. The glen is home to a number

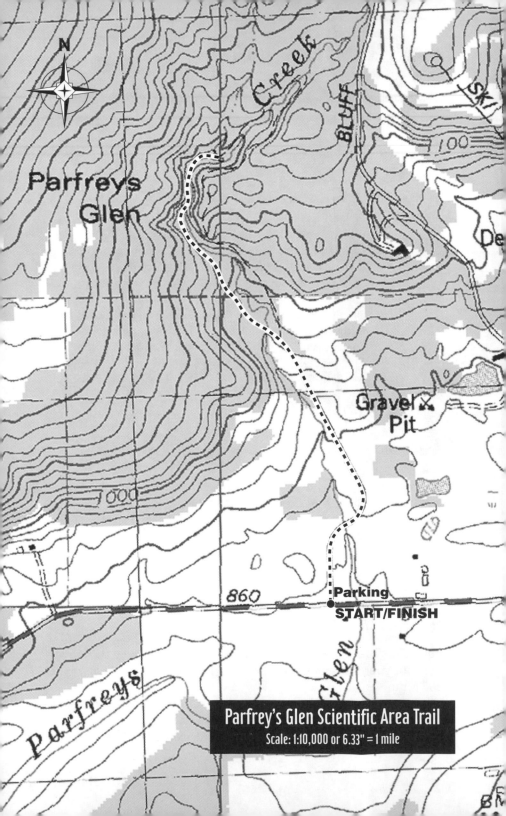

N

Parfreys
Glen

Creek

Bluff

SKI

100

De

Gravel
Pit

860

Parfreys

Glen

Parking
START/FINISH

Parfrey's Glen Scientific Area Trail
Scale: 1:10,000 or 6.33" = 1 mile

Directions at a glance

0.0 From the trailhead parking lot, go north on the unplowed road.

0.4 Continue straight (northwest) at the end of the road.

0.8 Continue straight (northeast) or turn around, depending on your willingness to cope with a short, twisting, very steep climb through fallen boulders.

0.9 Turn around at the overlook landing and return to the trailhead.

of very rare plants, so any deviation from the trail that packs down the snow might have an impact on their survival.

Amazing trees manage to cling to crevices in the glen's sheer walls. Green moss and multicolored lichens create a natural mural. The rock itself has a mysterious appearance. Layers of sandstone are separated by bands of rounded purple quartzite stones. These are evidence of ancient Cambrian seas that created beaches at different levels as they gradually filled the gorge.

Near the north end, the gorge becomes very narrow. You must navigate some very steep, narrow, twisting stretches to reach the end. I wouldn't advise this with traditional snowshoes. It is challenging even with modern shoes and a ski pole. One pole is better than two as it leaves a hand to grasp the stable, truncated boulders. Besides this last bit, the grade will have hardly been noticeable, even though you will have climbed 200 feet by the end.

How to get there

From the I–90/94 Merrimac exit, go west on WI 78 for 8 miles. Turn right (west) at County Highway DL and travel 2 miles to the Parfrey's Glen Natural Area parking lot entrance on the north side of the road.

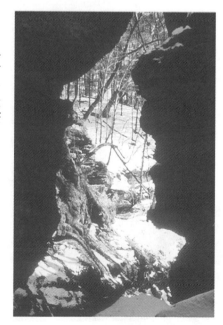

Near its end the glen narrows.

Wyalusing State Park Sugar Maple Trail

Bagley, Wisconsin

Type of trail:	
Also used by:	Hikers
Distance:	1.7 miles
Terrain:	Hilly with a few very steep sections
Trail difficulty:	Most difficult
Surface quality:	Ungroomed, hiker and snowshoer packed
Food and facilities:	Water is available in winter near the Nature Center, 0.7 mile north of the Park Office. There are outdoor toilets at the Sugar Maple Nature Trail picnic area. Several campsites are kept plowed for winter camping. All services are available in Prairie du Chien, 12 miles to the north. Check out the Black Angus for superior supper club fare.
Fees:	A daily or annual state park pass is required to enter via car.
Phone numbers:	Wyalusing State Park, (608) 996–2261; Prairie du Chien Tourism Council, (608) 326–8555 or (800) PDC–1673.
Equipment note:	Only modern snowshoes used with ski poles are recommended. There will be numerous, short, very steep, staired sections near Pictured Rock Cave.

The Sugar Maple Trail is your ticket to a wonder of winter. Deep in the recesses of a narrow niche in Wyalusing's 500-foot-high bluffs lies Pictured Rock Cave. In winter the sheltering dolomite overhang holds a beautiful frozen waterfall from rim to floor.

Following the loop in a clockwise direction will leave the cave for the last part. It will also make the 500-foot descent much easier, as you will be on an even grade. A red fox must make the trail part of its regular route. I followed its tracks, easily identified by the way they nearly form a single

A frozen waterfall at Pictured Rock Cave.

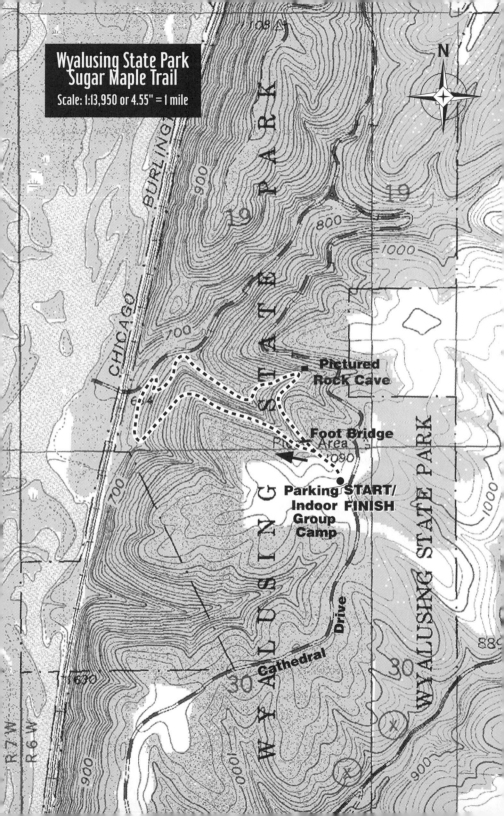

line. A pile of rabbit fur showed where the fox had caught its lunch.

Once in the bottomland you'll be across from the park's boat landing, which looks out on the myriad backwater sloughs of the Upper Mississippi River Wildlife and Fish Refuge.

The climb back up begins with steep switchbacks. It gets more tame for a while, then twisty, with steep stepped sections near Pictured Rock Cave and beyond. You may have to sidestep to make it into the cave. The frozen waterfall makes it all worthwhile.

Back on the Sugar Maple Trail after leaving the cave, the climb becomes a bit more gradual as you follow a bend around a point and into another bluff niche. As the niche narrows, you turn right onto a trail that descends sharply and crosses a small wooden bridge. This is the bridge you saw on your outbound leg. After a short steep climb you are headed back to the trailhead on the trail section you started on.

How to get there

From Prairie du Chien, take U.S. 18/WI 35 southeast for 7 miles. Or, traveling west from Fennimore, take U.S. 18 west for 22.2 miles. Turn southwest onto County Highway C. Go 3 miles to a "T" Intersection; turn right (west) onto County Highway CX for 1 mile. Turn right (north) into Wyalusing State Park. Turn left (west) just after the park office, where a brown-and-white sign indicates the direction to Homestead Group Camp and Ski Trails. Go 0.4 mile and turn left (south) at the Homestead Group Camp (other roads are unplowed). Turn left (south) after another 0.2 mile at a "T" intersection (the road to the right is unplowed). Pass the Picnic Area signed MAPLE SUGAR NATURE TRAIL. Go another 0.2 mile and bear right (west) to the Indoor Group Camp parking lot (the road to the left is unplowed). The Sugar Maple Trail is across the road from the parking area.

Wyalusing State Park Mississippi Ridge Trail
Bagley, Wisconsin

Type of trail:	▬▬▬
Distance:	3.2 miles round-trip
Terrain:	Flat to gently rolling
Trail difficulty:	Easy
Surface quality:	Groomed periodically, double tracked
Food and facilities:	See "Food and facilities" on page 64.
Fees:	A daily or annual state park pass is required to enter via car.
Events:	Candlelight Ski, second Friday in February.
Phone numbers:	Wyalusing State Park, (608) 996–2261; Prairie du Chien Tourism Council, (608) 326–8555 or (800) PDC–1673.

The Mississippi Ridge Trail is bound to be the easiest ski with the greatest view you will ever find. The two-way double tracked trail runs entirely in a deep hardwood forest. The most challenging part is a 5-foot dip into a little ravine. The tall maples hide the closely paralleling Cathedral Drive, which is unplowed in winter. If you ski late in the day, a low sun will cast bands of shadows across the drifted snow.

The overviews are as spectacular as the trail is tame. The first comes about half way along at a point deep in the woods. The second is at the southern end of the trail at the open picnic area. From both you'll look out across North America's mightiest river to the imposing bluffs of the Iowa shore.

Late one winter I witnessed the spectacular courting spiral of two bald eagles above the Mississippi bluffs. Soaring at bluff-top height,

N

CHIC

634

Picnic Area

1090

Parking

START/
FINISH

700

overlook

630

Cathedral Drive

30

30

R-6-W

900

1000

overlook

950

Picnic Area

WYALUSING STA

G

WYALUSING STA

**Wysalusing State Park
Mississippi Ridge Trail**
Scale: 1:10,980 or 5.78" = 1 mile

the couple moved close together. Then suddenly they were joined, free-falling together, spiraling hundreds of feet, separating just above the ground. It's a sight I'll never forget.

The park has two other ski trails, providing an additional 7 miles of skiing. The Turkey Hollow Trail has 120 feet of elevation and can be accessed directly from the north end of the Mississippi Ridge Trail.

How to get there

From Prairie du Chien, take U.S. 18/WI 35 southeast for 7 miles. Or, traveling west from Fennimore, take U.S. 18 west for 22.2 miles. Turn southwest onto County Highway C. Go 3 miles to a "T" Intersection; turn right (west) onto County Highway CX for 1 mile. Turn right (north) into Wyalusing State Park. Turn left (west) just after the park office, where a brown-and-white sign indicates the direction to Homestead Group Camp and Ski Trails. Go 0.4 mile and turn left (south) at the Homestead Group Camp (other roads are unplowed). Turn left (south) after another 0.2 mile at a "T" intersection (the road to the right is unplowed). Pass the Picnic Area signed MAPLE SUGAR NATURE TRAIL. Go another 0.2 mile and bear right (west) to the Indoor Group Camp parking lot (the road to the left is unplowed). The Mississippi Ridge Trail runs parallel on the south side of the road.

Skiers glide through the woods at Wyalusing State Park.

Justin Trails Doe Chase Trail
Sparta, Wisconsin

Type of trail:	▬ ◄
Also used by:	Skijorers and dogs
Distance:	2.2 miles
Terrain:	Hilly with steep sections
Trail difficulty:	Most difficult
Surface quality:	Groomed, single tracked, skate lane
Food and facilities:	Parking, indoor heated shelter and toilets, lodging, home-made chili, vending machines, breakfast for lodging guests, group lunches and dinners by arrangement, ski lessons, and snowshoe and ski rentals are available at the trailhead. All services are available in Sparta, 6 miles north.
Fees:	A daily or annual ski pass is required. Pay at the Eatery/Headquarters.
Events:	XC Ski Fest, second weekend in January; Dog Days Gone Wild skijoring event, first weekend in February; Moonlight Skiing, December through March.
Phone numbers:	Justin Trails, (608) 269–4522 or (800) 488–4521; Sparta Area Chamber of Commerce, (608) 269–4123 or (800) 354–BIKE (2453).
Internet:	www.justintrails.com

Donna and Don Justin seem to be on a mission. On their western Wisconsin farm they are making winter as much fun as possible without being too serious. Screaming people spinning down the tubing hill are one example. Letting skiers take their dogs along is another. Some enjoy the Scandinavian sport of skijoring, in which a dog and skier are joined with a tether. The dog leads and the skier follows—kind of like dogsledding without the sled.

Donna Justin and fellow skiers head for the trails.

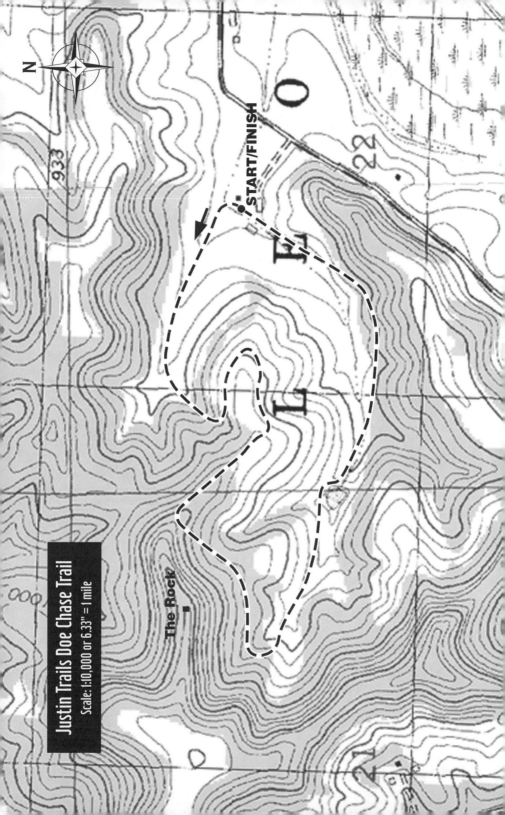

N

933

START/FINISH

The Rock

Justin Trails Doe Chase Trail
Scale: 1:10,000 or 6.33" = 1 mile

If your idea of fun also means great food, comfortable lodging, and an easy ski or snowshoe, you'll find it here. Do you get a kick out of the challenge of skiing up 200-foot bluffs and soaking up grand panoramic views? Try the Doe Chase Trail.

Justin Trails is centered around the pioneer farm that's been in Don Justin's family for generations. Recreation has replaced grazing on the 200-plus acres. It is also a playground for plentiful white-tailed deer and wild turkeys. Rooms in the farmhouse are one of the lodging options, along with three cottages. It's not rustic lodging; the emphasis is on comfort. Don and Donna have their own Web site and newsletter, which give details on the accommodations and all the activities year-round.

It is amazing how many people of different abilities take to the Doe Chase Trail. Skiers training for marathons attack the slopes. Recreational skiers sense the triumph of topping out. Great trail grooming makes it all possible and enjoyable. There is no substitute for good control on the downhills you'll find here.

Skiing counterclockwise from the farm on the mostly one-way loop, you get a warm-up during the first 0.3 mile as the trail gradually works its way up a narrowing valley. Turning up, 120 feet of elevation are gained in 0.1 mile. Next comes 0.5 mile of bluff-top cruising with glorious views as the trail swings around 180 degrees.

The downhill fun on Doe Chase is stretched out for more than 0.5 mile before you finally merge with the easy valley trails for a cool down back to the farm. There are another 4.5 miles of trail if Doe Chase has given you a taste for more.

Directions at a glance

0.0 Go north on the groomed two-way trail between the Eatery/Headquarters and the barn, following Doe Chase signs.

0.3 Turn left (southwest) on the one-way Doe Chase Trail as the Big Buck Run Trail merges from straight ahead.

1.4 Continue straight (southeast) as the Meadow Loop merges on the left.

1.6 Turn right (south) on Bambi Lane on the raised earthen dam as one-way Bambi Lane merges from straight ahead.

1.65 Turn left (east) on Bambi Lane/Doe Chase as Meadow Loop turns right. Follow to trailhead.

How to get there

From the I–90/WI 27 exit, go south for 4 miles and turn right (west) on County Highway J. Go 1.5 miles and turn right into the Justin Trails entrance.

Justin Trails Rock Trail

Sparta, Wisconsin

Type of trail:	
Distance:	1.7 miles
Terrain:	Hilly
Trail difficulty:	Most difficult
Surface quality:	Ungroomed, snowshoer packed
Food and facilities:	See "Food and facilities" on page 70.
Fees:	A daily or annual ski pass is required. Pay at the Eatery/Headquarters.
Phone numbers:	Justin Trails, (608) 269–4522 or (800) 488–4521; Sparta Area Chamber of Commerce, (608) 269–4123 or (800) 354–BIKE (2453).
Equipment note:	Modern snowshoes and one or two ski poles are recommended.

"I can make it to the top. I can make it to see the Rock." Keep telling yourself that as the snowshoe trail gets steeper and steeper. The payback will be a chance to rest on the Rock, a great place for a picnic lunch, as you gaze at the broadening valley 200 feet below. Don and Donna Justin believe in snowshoeing. They believe that snowshoeing can take people who don't want to ski hilly terrain to wonderful spots like the Rock overlook.

Separate snowshoe trails and snowshoe signs are two of the Justins' innovations. These features give the wonderful sense of solitude that makes snowshoeing a great way to get around. They reassure visitors that they are headed the right way and not on a detour to the North Pole. In addition to the Trail to the Rock, there are more than 3 miles of snowshoe trails on the property.

Don Justin shoes past a growth of sumac.

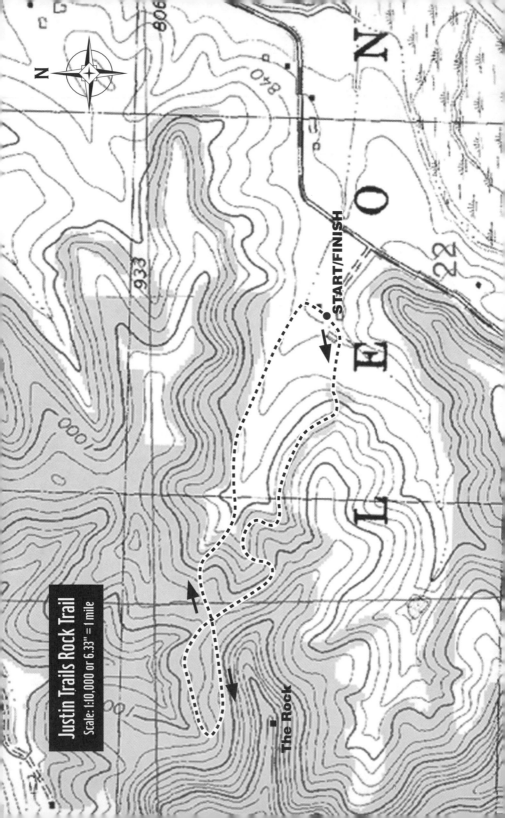

N

Justin Trails Rock Trail
Scale: 1:10,000 or 6.33" = 1mile

START/FINISH

The Rock

Directions at a glance

0.0 From the Eatery/Headquarters go around the south end of the barn, following the Rock signs.

0.2 Turn right (west) as the trail you are on goes straight.

0.4 Cross the Doe Chase ski trail.

0.7 Bear left (west) at a six-way intersection as the snowshoe trails cross the Big Buck Run ski trail.

1.1 Bear left (east) at a six-way intersection as the snowshoe trails cross the Big Buck Run ski trail.

1.2 Bear right (southeast) as the trail to the left goes uphill.

1.3 Continue straight (east) as the trail to the left goes uphill. Follow to trailhead.

Proceeding clockwise from the farm barn, follow the trail that strikes out across a field for the eastern point of one of the area's 200-foot bluffs. The perfectly contoured bluffs are a hallmark of the Driftless Area, the vast region of southwest Wisconsin untouched by glacial ice. After climbing a bit, the trail splits and follows the contour around through the deep aspen and maple forest. A swing to the south up a valley side notch gains most of the elevation, covering 100 feet in less than 0.1 mile.

The terrain is easier as you loop around to the Rock overlook. Take some time there to rest at this scenic spot. You may catch sight of the abundant wild turkeys or white-tailed deer. The trip back down is more direct as the trail heads into the valley. The last stretch runs along the ski trail. Be sure to wave.

How to get there

From the I–90/WI 27 exit, go south for 4 miles and turn right (west) on County Highway J. Go 1.5 miles and turn right into the Justin Trails entrance.

Black River State Forest Smreaker Trails

Millston, Wisconsin

Type of trail: ▬ ◄

Distance: 5.2 miles

Terrain: Hilly and rolling, with some very steep sections

Trail difficulty: Most difficult

Surface quality: Groomed periodically, single tracked, skate lane

Food and facilities: Parking and outdoor toilets are at the trailhead. Outdoor toilets and an Adirondack shelter are on the backside of the loop. A restaurant and motel are sometimes open in Millston. All services are available in Black River Falls, 12 miles northwest, where there are a number of economy and upscale motels near the I–94/WI 54 interchange, including the Arrowhead Lodge with a restaurant, indoor pool, whirlpool, and sauna. Molly's restaurant on Main Street serves the local microbrew, Pioneer Beer. You can stop in the brewery 2 blocks south of Main at Fourth and Pierce. It's located in the town's original brewery building; sampling is encouraged.

Fees: A daily or annual state park pass is required to enter the forest via car. Pay at the booth or self-pay station at the trailhead or purchase a pass at the DNR headquarters in Black River Falls.

Phone numbers: Black River State Forest, (715) 284–1400; Black River Area Chamber of Commerce, (715) 284–4658.

This is one tough and beautiful trail system. You'll see the ridges of Black River State Forest as you travel I–94. These remnant sandstone hills rise up 300 feet out of the thick woods. Your ski on the Smreaker Trails will include going up and down one of these babies. It won't be all work—once on top you'll have fantastic views as you roll along the ridge top. An exciting downhill run will take you back onto rolling trails in the lowland forest.

Though the trail starts out gradual, you are going uphill from the very beginning. Things really get steep when you turn onto the Ridge Trail, where you'll climb 300 feet in less than 0.25 mile. You'll travel the loop counterclockwise; all trails are one-way except for the Link Trail. If you feel the need for a warm-up before taking on the ridge, you can do the South Trail, which adds 1.5 miles to your ski and returns you to the start.

Once on top of the ridge the work isn't over. You'll roll along on the narrow crest line for 1.25 miles, losing and gaining 90 to 170 feet of ele-

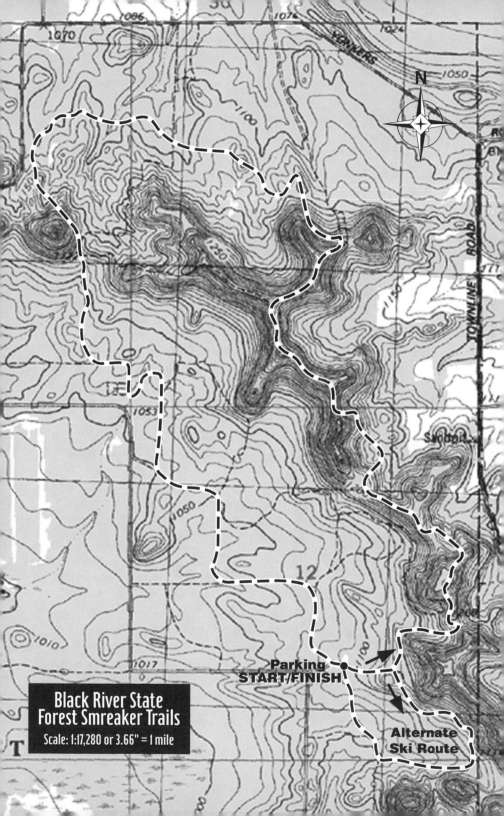

Black River State Forest Smreaker Trails
Scale: 1:17,280 or 3.66" = 1 mile

Parking
START/FINISH

Alternate
Ski Route

vation five times. In some places the ridge is knifelike, dropping away steeply on either side. You can see the vast evergreen forest far below as you cruise through the upland oak, maple, and birch hardwood forest. On a good day it's one of those "I'm lucky to be alive" experiences.

All of the downhill run-outs up on the ridge are straight except for the last one. There, the trail swings to the east on a side ridge then drops away suddenly into a sharp left turn and a long steep downhill. Soon you'll be rolling over easy terrain as you glide back through the pines to the trailhead.

How to get there

From I–94 at the County Highway O/Millston exit, travel northeast 0.1 mile and turn left on North Settlement Road. Go another 3.7 miles and turn right (east) on Smreaker Road. Travel 2.2 miles to the Smreaker Trail parking area on the left.

Snow frosting coats trees near and far.

Black River State Forest Pigeon Creek Trail
Millston, Wisconsin

Type of trail:	
Also used by:	Hikers
Distance:	5.6 miles round-trip
Terrain:	Flat
Trail difficulty:	Easy
Surface quality:	Ungroomed; hiker, skier, and snowshoer packed
Food and facilities:	See "Food and facilities" on page 76.
Fees:	A daily or annual state park pass is required to enter the forest via car. Pay at the booth or self-pay station at the trailhead or purchase a pass at the DNR headquarters in Black River Falls.
Phone numbers:	Black River State Forest, (715) 284–1400; Black River Area Chamber of Commerce, (715) 284–4658.

The Pigeon Creek Trail is a nice out-and-back jaunt through the lowland woods of Black River Falls State Forest. It's a good, easy alternative to skiing the ridges if the conditions are icy, or just a pleasant, flat trek at anytime. And because it's an out-and-back trail, you can snowshoe or ski just as far as you feel like.

The vast Black River State Forest covers 66,000 acres of mixed hardwood, evergreen, and marsh. The hard oak and maple grow on the 400-foot mounds and ridges. The lowland is more suitable for red, white, and jack pine. Although there were early attempts at farming the land, the sandy soil only produced back break and heart break.

The trail begins with a short stretch on the straight earthen dike that holds back the waters of Pigeon Creek, creating a small lake. Rounding

Easy going on the flat Pigeon Creek Trail.

Black River State Forest
Pigeon Creek Trail
Scale: 1:21,660 or 2.92" = 1 mile

START/FINISH

Parking

Pigeon Creek Flowage

Campground

Sharptail Flowage

Directions at a glance

0.0   From the Pigeon Creek Campground parking lot, go southeast on the Pigeon Creek Flowage earthen dam, following brown-and-white mountain bike silhouette signs.

0.3   Continue straight (southeast) on the dam as a mountain bike trail spur turns right.

2.8   Turn around at Smreaker Road and return to the trailhead.

the south end, you plunge into the thick pine forest. Ahead you will see the steep ridge the other ski trails are on. Snowshoeing is not allowed on those ski trails. Considering the grades you would hit on the ridge, it's just as well.

How to get there

From I–94 at the County Highway O/Millston exit, travel northeast 0.1 mile and turn left on North Settlement Road. Travel 2 miles to the Pigeon Creek Campground entrance on the right.

Perrot State Park Perrot Ridge Trail
Trempealeau, Wisconsin

Type of trail:	⬤⬤⬤⬤
Also used by:	Hikers
Distance:	1.4 miles
Terrain:	Hilly with very steep sections
Trail difficulty:	Most difficult
Surface quality:	Ungroomed, hiker and snowshoer packed
Food and facilities:	Parking and outdoor toilets are at the trailhead. The park Nature Center, 1.5 miles west, is open on weekends and has water and flush toilets. Most services are available in Trempealeau, 2 miles east, including motels and the not to be missed Trempealeau Hotel, where you can get a walnut burger.
Fees:	A daily or annual park pass is required to enter via car. Pay at the entrance booth self-pay station.
Phone numbers:	Perrot State Park, (608) 534–6409; Trempealeau County Clerk's Office, (715) 538–2311.
Equipment note:	Modern snowshoes will be needed; at least one ski pole is recommended.

La montagne qui tremp à l'eau. The mountain dipping in the water. Trempealeau Mountain is unique. In the entire 2,400-mile length of the

Mississippi River, it is the only hill. Separated from the shore by a change in the channel, it has been a gathering place since people first canoed this great river highway. Perrot (PAIR-oh) State Park is one of the most beautiful and historic places in Wisconsin. When you reach the top of the 280-foot climb you'll agree it's one of the most scenic too.

Your snowshoe trek begins at one of the park's Hopewell

The frozen Mississippi River lies in the distance below Perrot Ridge.

Perrot State Park
Perrot Ridge Trail

Scale: 1:10,000 or 6.33" = 1 mile

Directions at a glance

0.0 From the east side of the trailhead parking lot, go south to the Hopewell Mound marker, then swing northeast, following the brown-and-white hiker silhouettes and Perrot Ridge Trail signs.

0.1 Cross the park entrance road.

0.4 Turn right (east) as the ravine splits. This point is not signed; the way straight ahead is not cleared.

0.7 Turn left (west) onto the groomed ski trail signed REED'S RUN. The trail straight ahead is closed. The trail on the right is one-way, signed DO NOT ENTER.

1.1 Turn left (southwest) at the overlook bench and follow the Perrot Ridge Trail sign. The ski trail turns right at this point.

1.3 Cross the park entrance road and return to the trailhead.

mounds. Two thousand years ago the Hopewell Culture spread from its Ohio base throughout mid-America's river systems. It brought the beginnings of agriculture; a vast trading network dealing in Rocky Mountain obsidian, Lake Superior copper, and Florida marine shells; and a tradition of burial that included wonderful art objects. Trempealeau County was a Hopewell center. Upwards of 2,000 mounds and earthworks have been identified here.

The Perrot Ridge Trail is best snowshoed in a counterclockwise direction. From the Hopewell mound you'll parallel the road for a bit then turn inland, heading up a beautiful ravine. A narrow, old stone bridge should be crossed with caution if icy. As the ravine splits, you'll begin the long climb up Perrot Ridge. Topping out, signs direct you onto the ski trail marked REED'S RUN. Coming out of the woods, you'll have a superb view of the Mississippi, the bluffs beyond, and the railroad trains that run up and down the valley—a grand day of snowshoeing by any standard.

How to get there

From WI 35/Main Street and Third Street in Trempealeau, where WI 35 turns left (east) on Third Street, continue straight (south) on Main Street for 2 blocks and turn right (west) on First Street. Follow it for 1.9 miles and turn left into the small parking lot just past the park entrance station.

Perrot State Park Cedar Glade/Perrot Ridge Trails

Trempealeau, Wisconsin

Type of trail:	▬▬▬
Also used by:	Snowshoers on one short stretch
Distance:	5 miles
Terrain:	Hilly with very steep sections
Trail difficulty:	Most difficult
Surface quality:	Groomed periodically, mainly single tracked, double tracked on two-way sections
Food and facilities:	See "Food and facilities" on page 82.
Fees:	A daily or annual park pass is required to enter via car. Pay at the entrance booth self-pay station.
Events:	Candlelight Ski, first Saturday in January.
Phone numbers:	Perrot State Park, (608) 534–6409; Trempealeau County Clerk's Office, (715) 538–2311.

When it comes to steep ups and downs, trails don't come any tougher than the ridge loops at Perrot. They are at the high end of the most difficult scale. Even expert skiers would be wise to ski them only in excellent conditions. If it's icy, get out the snowshoes (see page 82) or try skiing the easy 2 mile Bay Trail.

That said, challenging trails can be rewarding. Perrot is a prime example. You'll ski through a beautiful white pine, birch, and maple forest and have a fantastic view of the Mississippi Valley for your hard work. And, hey, steep downhills are exciting. If you make it through the sharp right-hander coming off of Chicken Breast Bluff, you should win a medal. After falling the first time, I herringboned back up twice to try again. I couldn't stay on my feet on those attempts either.

Starting at the Nature Center, which makes a nice warming house when it's

Single-track skiing through the woods at Perrot State Park.

Perrot State Park Cedar
Glade/Perrot Ridge Trails

Scale: 1:15,280 or 4.15" = 1 mile

Directions at a glance

0.0 From the park Nature Center, follow the two-way groomed ski trail east then south through open areas to the park office.

0.2 Turn left (east) at the park office onto the Brady's Bluff Trail, following blue-and-white skier silhouette signs. YOU ARE HERE map signs are at some intersections.

0.6 Turn left (north) onto the one-way Wilber's Trail.

1.5 Continue straight (south) onto the Cedar Glade Trail and begin climbing. The sign says TOW ROPE HILL.

1.7 Continue straight (southeast) on the Cedar Glade Trail as the Prairie Trail splits off to the right.

3.4 Bear left (west) after a long climb as the Prairie Trail merges from the right. Follow the REED'S RUN sign.

3.8 Continue around Perrot Ridge and to the right (north) at the scenic overlook.

4.3 Turn left (west) at a "T" intersection onto a two-way trail. Follow to trailhead.

open on weekends, you've got a mile to warm up before the first big climb. The loop circuits the bluffs in a clockwise direction. The TOW ROPE HILL sign and black diamond rating at the start of the Cedar Glade Trail should tell you what's ahead. You'll climb 150 feet in 0.2 mile.

On the ridge you're in for a roller coaster ride to the Chicken Breast Bluff turn. Once around it, you'll shoot down into Valley Run for a sweet 0.5 mile between two steep ridges. Then it's up again, this time for 250 feet in a 0.3 mile. At the top you are up on Perrot Ridge, a bow-shaped feature facing the Mississippi.

Soon you're skiing up and down for nearly 0.5 mile along the inside of the Perrot Ridge bow on Reed's Run. The trail comes out of the woods at a scenic overlook of the river and bluffs on the Minnesota side. All this skiing excitement ends with a 0.2 mile, 100-foot drop back down to the lowland. Believe me, skiing Perrot earns you bragging rights at the Trempealeau Hotel bar.

How to get there

From WI 35/Main Street and Third Street in Trempealeau, where WI 35 turns left (east) on Third Street, continue straight on Main Street for 2 blocks and turn right (west) on First Street. Follow it for 3.25 miles into the park to the Nature Center parking lot.

Standing Rocks Park Loggers Loop
Amherst, Wisconsin

Type of trail: ▬▬ ◀

Distance: 4.9 miles

Terrain: Rolling

Trail difficulty: More difficult

Surface quality: Groomed, single tracked, skate lane

Food and facilities: Parking at the trailhead. Heated indoor shelter, toilets, snacks, and ski rentals at the chalet when open (weekends and many in-season midweek days). Outdoor toilets are at the south end of Tower Road. Some services are available in Amherst, 7 miles east, including sandwiches at the Club Orlo tavern (ask for the atomic horseradish). All services are available in Stevens Point, 11 miles west, including ski retail and repair.

Fees: A daily or annual trail ticket is required to enter via car. Pay at the chalet or self-pay station at the trailhead.

Events: Standing Rocks Nordski Rendezvous, third Saturday in January.

Phone numbers: Portage County Parks Department, (715) 346–1433; Stevens Point Chamber of Commerce, (715) 344–1940.

Standing Rocks—home of the glacial erratic and the skiing fanatic. They used to sell T-shirts with that motto on the front. Glacial erratics are huge granite boulders—the standing rocks—that the Green Bay ice sheet rolled to its western edge. Beyond the park, just a short distance west, the terrain flattens almost completely. For you, the skiing fanatic, the important things are that the big rocks are not on the trail and that the glacier left some excellent skiing terrain. A commitment to good grooming is another strong point at Standing Rocks; the comfortable chalet adds to the experience.

Standing Rocks' trail system has evolved over the past fifteen years from a few basic loops to today's explosion-in-a-spaghetti-factory milieu of skiing options. The Loggers Loop is one of the venerable routes that offers the kind of moderate cross-country experience the park was known for before trails named Gut Buster, The Wall, and Last Thrill were added.

Skiing counterclockwise on the mostly one-way loops, you plunge into a forest of maple, aspen, and pine. After a warm-up on easy terrain for 0.3 mile, the trail turns north into a fast, but not too steep, 50-foot downhill run. A turn to the west puts you on an even slope where the trail regains that elevation in 0.1 mile. The trail is gently rolling for the next 0.5 mile before a similar down and up just west of Tower Road.

You are now on the classic Loggers Loop, an easy skiing, rolling 2-mile stretch. It has enough elevation change to get your heart rate up, as well as some fun, gradual downhills and enough flat to let you relax and enjoy the scenery. White-tailed deer are plentiful, so keep your eyes peeled.

There are an incredible number of blue trail and shortcut options on the western part of the Loggers Loop. You can try any of these for a taste of tougher climbs and turns. These typically add 0.25 to a 0.5 mile to the trip, except for the last blue trail option, which sends you down the fast 70-foot Last Thrill run and actually cuts off some distance.

If you start from the chalet instead of the trailhead, you'll add 0.65 mile to your ski. All in all, there are another 4 miles of skiing at Standing Rocks. Stay tuned. There is sure to be more spaghetti in the future.

Monstrous glacial boulders gave Standing Rocks its name.

How to get there

From U.S. 10 at Amherst, go west on County Highway B for 4.5 miles and turn left on County Highway K. Go south 1 mile. Turn right on Standing Rocks Road and go west 1.2 miles to the Standing Rocks County Park trailhead parking lot or chalet entrance road on the right.

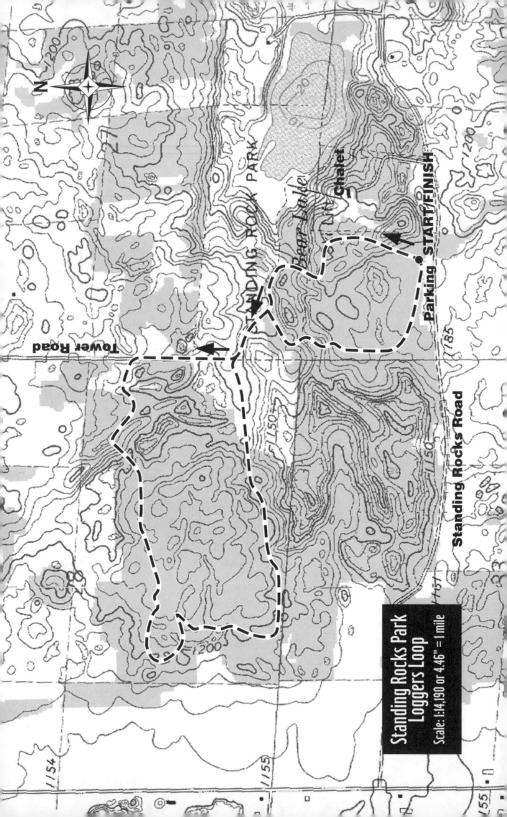

**Standing Rocks Park
Loggers Loop**

Scale: 1:14,190 or 4.46" = 1 mile

START/FINISH

Parking

Chalet

Bear Lake

STANDING ROCK PARK

Tower Road

Standing Rocks Road

Directions at a glance

0.0 From the trailhead signboard, go north, bearing right on the one-way groomed Loggers Loop. Follow red color-coded marker posts. YOU ARE HERE map signs are at most intersections.

0.5 Turn right (north) at a four-way intersection onto the Red and Blue Trails as the Green Trail continues straight.

0.6 Turn left (northwest) on the wide one-way Red Trail.

0.8 Bear right (northwest) on a wide two-way trail as the Red Trail splits after a downhill run through the Big Pines section.

1.0 Turn right (north) on a wide one-way trail as the Red Trail splits again with the two-way trail going left. This is the Tower Road Trail section, where the Red and Blue Trails join.

1.3 Turn left (west) off the road into the woods on a narrower trail. From this point to the next cue, take the right trail at all intersections, always following the red markers.

3.4 Bear left (northeast) on the red Pine Ridge section as the Blue Trail splits right.

4.0 Bear right (east) on the wide two-way Red Trail as the one-way Red Trail turns left.

4.2 Turn right (southwest) on the one-way Red Trail as the outbound Red Trail merges on the left.

4.5 Turn right (west) at a four-way intersection on the red, blue, and green trail as the green trail merges on the left and a red and blue trail continues straight. Follow to trailhead.

Iola Norseman Black Trail

Iola, Wisconsin

Type of trail: ▬ ◄

Distance: 3.5 miles

Terrain: Rolling to hilly with steep sections

Trail difficulty: Most difficult

Surface quality: Groomed frequently, single tracked, skate lane

Food and facilities: Parking, enclosed heated shelter, snacks, and indoor toilets are at the trailhead. Iola has most basic services. All services, including ski retail, rental, and repair, are found in Waupaca, 18 miles south. Check out the Wheelhouse for outrageous pizza.

Fees: A daily trail fee or an annual membership is required.

Events: The Iola Norseman Challenge cross-country ski races, third Sunday in January. The first weekend of February is the usual date for jumping competitions.

Phone numbers: Iola Winter Sports Club, (715) 445–3411; Waupaca Area Chamber of Commerce, (715) 258–7343 or (888) 417–4040.

Want to join a 90-year-old ski club? For about the equivalent of a downhill ski ticket or a round of golf you can become a member of the Iola Winter Sports Club. Skiers have been jumping at Norseman Hill since the club was formed in 1910. Today there are five ski jumps, including a new 130-foot-high 60-meter jump.

For those who don't have the courage to get airborne, there are wonderful cross-country ski trails that are groomed with state-of-the-art equipment. You won't find better grooming anywhere. You don't have to be a club member to enjoy the trails; paying a daily fee opens up this cross-country wonderland. It is amazing how a town with barely more than a thousand residents supports a facility like this. It's a credit to the community's Norwegian heritage.

The clubhouse alone is enough to make the area attractive. It is open on weekends and most weeknights, when a 2.5-mile loop is lighted for

Directions at a glance

0.0 From the trailhead clubhouse, ski west on the very wide two-way groomed trail. After 30 yards, angle off to the right (northwest) on the one-way, uphill trail, following black diamond signs and making right turns at all intersections.

3.2 Bear right at a four-way intersection onto the very wide two-way trail and follow it back to the trailhead.

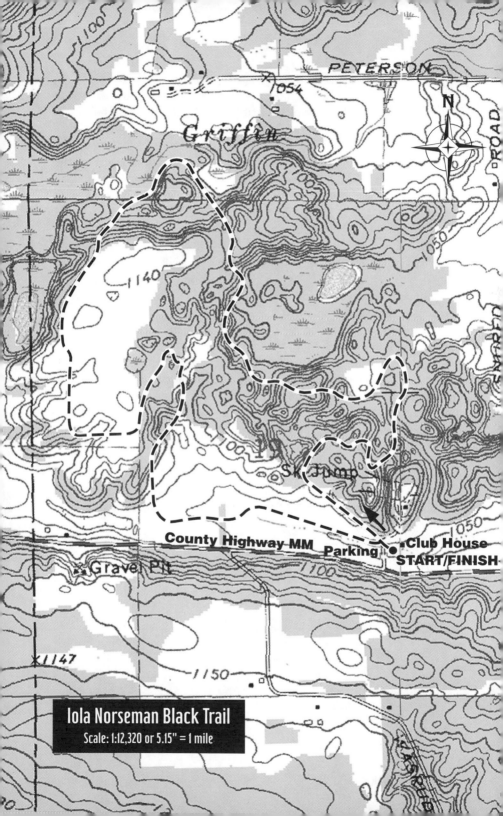

PETERSON

X 1054

Griffin

N

ROAD

1050

1140

Ski Jump

County Highway MM   Parking

Club House
START/FINISH

1050

Gravel Pit

1100

X 1147

1150

ROAD

Iola Norseman Black Trail
Scale: 1:12,320 or 5.15" = 1 mile

night skiing. There are another 3 miles of skiing on other easier loops.

I have a wonderful early twentieth century postcard showing a woman on wooden skis dressed in a scarf, jacket, and a full skirt. Shot in a studio, there is a painted winter-scene backdrop and a little evergreen in the foreground. The adoring expression on the model's face tells it all. There was romance in skiing then. There is romance in skiing today. Maybe you should join the club and be a part of the rich skiing tradition.

The skiing challenge begins quickly as the trail climbs up from the clubhouse. The first 0.5 mile of trails winds its way through a thick oak and maple forest to the top of the jumping hill, an 80-foot climb. As you might imagine, this is followed by an exciting downhill run, on which I have broken two skis by misjudging the fast left-hand turn. This is just the beginning.

The trail system is very compact and has too many intersections to fully describe in the Directions at a glance section. The Black Trail is easily followed, however. In addition to following the black diamond signs, just make all of your turns right-handers and you can't go wrong. If you like to snowshoe, a section of the Ice Age Trail runs through the area. Look for yellow-topped signposts.

Most of the many Black Trail climbs and descents are in the 50- to 60-foot range. It seems that challenging skiers on the downhill runs was a goal of the trail designer. There are easy stretches along the northernmost bend, through fields to the west, and in the pine forest on the final leg. Just when you think it's safe to lollygag along, it hits you with another tough downhill run that would make a Norwegian proud.

How to get there
From WI 49, 3.4 miles north of Iola, go west on County Highway MM for 1.4 miles to the Iola Winter Sports Club parking lot on the right.

Skiers have jumped at Norseman Hill for ninety years.

Nine Mile Forest 6K Trail

Wausau, Wisconsin

Type of trail: ▬ ◀

Distance: 4.1 miles

Terrain: Rolling

Trail difficulty: More difficult

Surface quality: Groomed frequently, single tracked, skate lane

Food and facilities: Parking, a heated indoor shelter building, and toilets are at the trailhead. All services are available in Wausau, including ski retail and rental.

Fees: A daily or annual ski pass is required. Pay at the shelter desk when open or the self-pay station at the parking lot.

Events: Snekkevik Classic cross-country ski race, first Saturday in January; Badger State Games cross-country ski races, first weekend in February.

Phone numbers: Marathon County Forestry Department, (715) 847–5267; Wausau Area Convention and Visitors Council, (800) 235–WSAU or (715) 845–6231.

The ski trails that snake through 4,755-acre Nine Mile Forest have grown and steadily improved over the past 25 years. Trail sections are now identified by letters. and YOU ARE HERE map signs are frequent. The tougher trails used to have names like Bushwacker and Zimbric's Zig-Zag. Local skiers still know the trails by the old names and I chose to include them in the directions. I call this loop the 6K Trail because it is about 6 kilometers long. At a ski area named Nine Mile Forest, a trail named 6K seems appropriate.

The name is a bit nondescript, but the skiing is wonderful. Nine Mile Forest is popular with local skiers and visitors alike. The trails are used for the cross-country races of the Badger State Games each February. These races are among the most heavily attended events in the annual winter sports festival. The Snekkevik Classic is a traditional ski striding race held earlier in the season. One of the oldest races in the Midwest, it was inspired by Asbjorn Snekkevik, a Norwegian who showed the people in Wausau how much fun cross-country could be in the early 1970s.

Part of Nine Mile's popularity for racing or touring is due to the large, comfortable shelter building. It is a great place to socialize and watch skiers glide by the large windows. Another part of the appeal is the challenging terrain. A nasty 250-foot-high ridge runs through the area. The 6K Trail will be a lot easier because it avoids the ridge entirely.

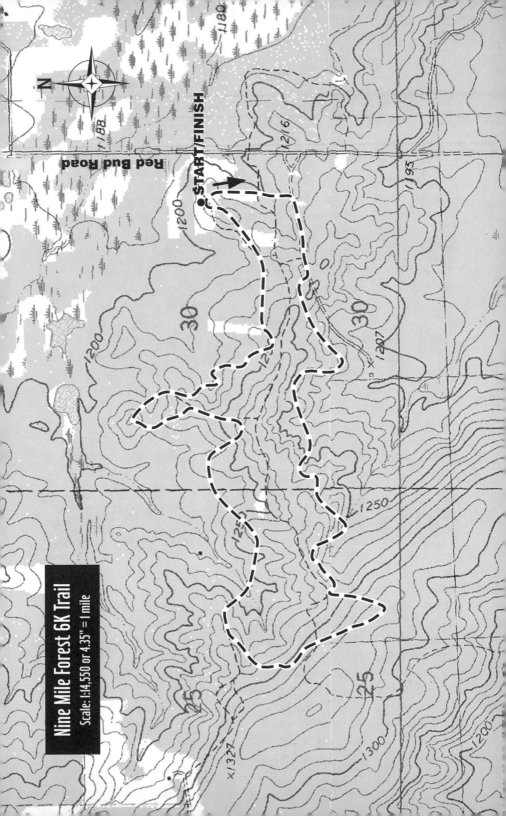

Directions at a glance

0.0 From the south side of the shelter building, go south on the very wide groomed trail. YOU ARE HERE map signs are at many intersections.

0.2 Turn right (west) on Main Street.

0.4 Turn right (north) on a link trail and make an immediate left (west) on Tenderfoot.

1.2 Turn right (west) on Reichl's Ridge. There is a YOU ARE HERE map sign at this intersection.

1.7 Turn right (northwest) on Trail V.

1.9 Continue straight (northwest) onto Sourdough Trail as trail Y merges on the right. Ignore several shortcut trails, following Sourdough Trail back to the trailhead.

This one-way clockwise loop gives a nice taste of the skiing at Nine Mile. After 0.5 mile of gradual uphill, the trails begin to roll over terrain with 50 to 70 feet of relief. This makes for some challenge, but lacks the intimidation of the ridge. Downhills are moderate and turns are easy in fresh snow conditions. If you handle this loop easily, there are another 10 miles of trail here. Most are real tough. Your first somewhat challenging downhill is a sharp right hander at 0.65 mile. It may surprise you as the trail has been so easy to this point. It will be easy again until 1.2 miles, when another not-so-sharp right-hand turn appears at the end of a long gradual downhill run. Soon you are on the Sourdough Trail (Trail Q), the longest stretch on the loop. Expect long gradual climbs and descents until 3.4 miles, when a short downhill takes you into a sharp left-hand turn just to keep you on your toes. From there it is an easy gently rolling cruise back to the start/finish.

How to get there
From the I–39/County Highway N exit, go west on County Highway N for 3.6 miles. Turn left (south) on Red Bud Road for 1.8 miles to the Nine Mile Forest Ski Trails entrance on the right.

Rib Mountain State Park Yellow Trail

Wausau, Wisconsin

Type of trail:	🐾
Also used by:	Hikers
Distance:	2.9 miles
Terrain:	Hilly with very steep sections
Trail difficulty:	Most difficult
Surface quality:	Ungroomed, snowshoer and hiker packed
Food and facilities:	The park office provides shelter when open and parking anytime. Outdoor toilets are located near the trailhead and Sunrise Lookout. All services are available in Wausau, including snowshoe retail and rental.
Fees:	A daily or annual state park pass is required to enter the park by car. Pay at the park office (if open) or self-pay station at the door.
Events:	Badger State Games Mountaineer 5 Mile Run/Tour snowshoe event, first Sunday in February.
Phone numbers:	Rib Mountain State Park, (715) 842–2522; Wausau Area Convention and Visitors Council, (800) 235–WSAU or (715) 845–6231.
Equipment note:	Bear Paw traditional or modern snowshoes with at least one ski pole are recommended.

Rib Mountain is marked by contrast. To the north of this narrow ridge, open slopes and ski lifts overlook the City of Wausau. The south side is wild on its slopes and beyond. It is into this beautiful forest that you will point your snowshoes. The hill is very steep; you'll lose and gain more than 500 feet of elevation. A bright winter sun makes the trek more pleasant. You can't be faulted for pausing to soak up some rays—and to let your pulse rate drop. Bounding white-tailed deer will make you stop too. Deer are thick in this uncrowded park. It's likely they will be your only companions.

Rib Mountain itself is a geological anomaly. Rising about 800 feet above the level of the Wisconsin River, it is a remnant of the area's mountainous past. Technically it is called a monadnock, a mass of tough quartzite that has resisted a billion years of erosion and a million years of glaciation. As you hike down you will catch glimpses of another monadnock, Mosinee Hill, in the distance. Once back on top the trail skirts around Sunrise Lookout and Cobbler's Nob, where blue-gray quartzite rocks poke out above the surface.

Rib Mountain is the only state park at present that marks trails specifically for snowshoeing. Combination snowshoe and hiker signs are placed frequently along the trail either at intersections or as confidence markers along the way. Trail names are not included. With the abundance of trails, things can get a bit confusing. The drastic elevation change helps you determine which trail is which; the park map shows the location of each signpost accurately.

The wilderness feeling and the abundance of trails (there are another 5 miles of them) make Rib Mountain a great destination for snowshoeing. It is the site of the Mountaineer 5 Mile Run/Tour, one of the snowshoe events in the annual Badger State Games, a winter sports festival.

Trails are two-way. I suggest traveling in a clockwise direction, leaving the climb for the third leg. When I snowshoed, 8 inches of fresh snow had fallen the night before. There were no snowshoe tracks beyond the first intersection. There were ski tracks though. Someone had Telemarked between the trees all the way down the steep, narrow, twisting trail. I kept expecting to find a huge sitzmark, but each turn had been executed perfectly. As I turned west to continue the loop, the tracks kept going down. It was an amazing feat, but I doubt it will make it as an event in the Badger State Games.

Leaving the tracks of the adventurous skier behind I headed west in pristine, unbroken powder snow, first on flatland,

Sunrise at Rib Mountain.

then on a moderately steepening climb. After a sharp right turn I immediately faced the big challenge of the loop. Heading north, 375 feet are gained in only 0.4 mile. That works out to a one-in-five grade. The ski poles come in handy here, though even with them you will be huffing and puffing. Who says snowshoeing isn't an aerobic sport?

As you reach the park benches near the Green Trail intersection, you may need to sit for a minute and marvel at the terrain you've climbed. There is some uphill left, but it will seem a piece of cake after the long haul. The twists and turns around Sunrise Lookout and Cobbler's Nob make a very scenic stretch. Beyond you will go up and down about 50 feet several times before reaching the start/finish.

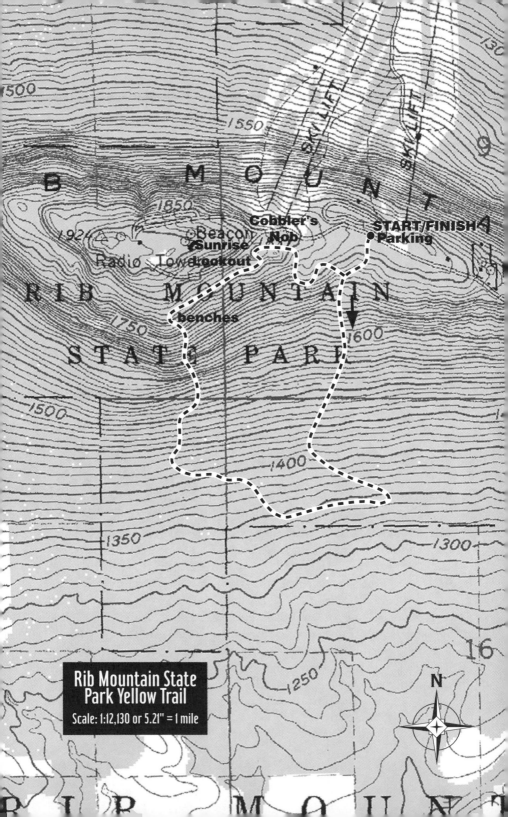

Rib Mountain State Park Yellow Trail
Scale: 1:12,130 or 5.21" = 1 mile

Directions at a glance

0.0   Look for the brown-and-white Family Campground sign across the park road from the park office. The sign arrow points north, but the Yellow Trail begins there. Go south, following blue-and-white snowshoe signs. You are on the Lower East Yellow Trail.

0.1   Turn left (south) downhill as a trail merges on the right. Both are part of the Lower East Yellow Trail (no name sign).

0.2   Turn right (southwest) as a trail goes left. Both are part of the Lower Middle Yellow Trail (no name sign).

0.5   Turn left (southeast) as an unmarked trail goes right (a dead end).

0.7   Turn right (west) on the Lower West Yellow Trail (no name sign) as the trail you are on continues east.

1.4   Continue straight (west) at a gated trail on the left signed NOT A HIKING TRAIL.

1.5   Turn right (northeast) on the Lower West Yellow Trail (no name sign) and begin climbing sharply.

1.9   Turn right (north) on the Green Trail (no name sign) just after passing two benches.

2.2   Turn right (east) at Sunrise Lookout Rock on the Lower East Yellow Trail (no name sign).

2.8   Turn left (northeast) on the Lower East Yellow Trail (no name sign) and return to the trailhead.

How to get there

From I–39/U.S. 51 at the County Highway N exit, go west 0.2 mile and turn right on Park Road. Follow it to the top of Rib Mountain and the park office parking lot.

Dells of the Eau Claire River/Bluff Trails

Hogarty, Wisconsin

Type of trail: ⊙⊙⊙⊙

Also used by: Hikers

Distance: 1.5 miles

Terrain: Flat with a few steep sections

Trail difficulty: More difficult

Surface quality: Ungroomed, snowshoer and hiker packed

Food and facilities: Parking and clean outdoor toilets are at the trailhead. All services are available in Wausau, 19 miles west, including snowshoe retail and rental.

Phone numbers: Wausau Area Convention and Visitors Council, (800) 235-WSAU or (715) 845-6231; Marathon County Park Department, (715) 847-5235.

Equipment note: Use modern snowshoes and at least one ski pole.

One of the most photographed small parks in Wisconsin, the Dells of the Eau Claire has the always fascinating combination of swift water tumbling over jumbled rock into a sheer-walled gorge. It is an incredibly scenic place in any season. In winter, the waterfall flows silently inside an encasement of ice. Mounds of snow round the rough contours of massive, angular volcanic rock, and only occasional swirling open pools show that the river still flows.

The author snowshoes past the truncated rocks at the Dells of the Eau Claire.

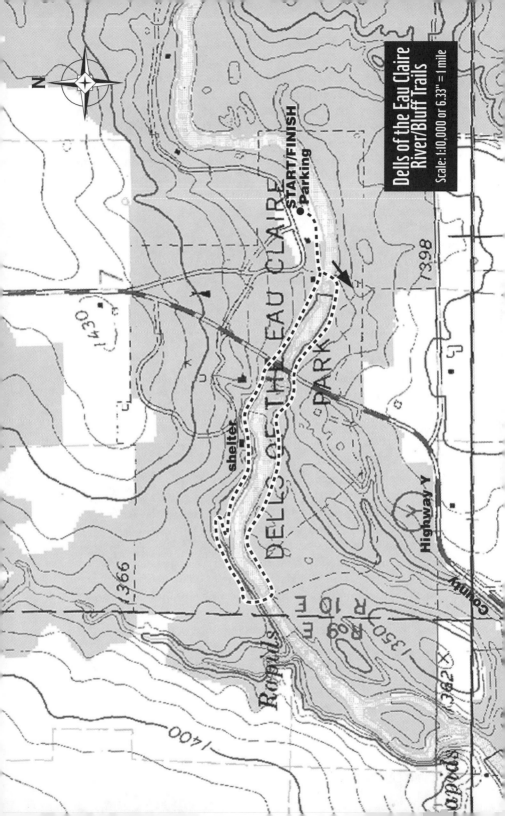

Dells of the Eau Claire
River/Bluff Trails

Scale: 1:10,000 or 6.33" = 1 mile

N

START/FINISH
● Parking

DELLS OF THE EAU CLAIRE PARK

shelter

Highway Y

Rapids
1350 R9 E R10 E
1366
1400

1362 X

County

1430
1398
7

You have a good chance of having all this beauty to yourself in winter. Traveling clockwise on the two-way trails, you first cross a footbridge over a small dam for a fine view of the frozen rapids downstream.

Turning west, the trail winds through thick riverside hemlocks. Upended by a windstorm, one of these shows its intricate root system, which came up as the tree went down.

Along the river the trail crosses a short stone bridge with no side rails. Though only about 10 feet long, the 30-inch-wide bridge is one of the reasons for using modern snowshoes with crampons for traction. Another reason comes shortly thereafter, when you need to climb over snowbanks to cross County Highway Y. After crossing, you must descend several short stretches of snow- and ice-covered stone steps, which will require sidestepping.

Going downstream, you have beautiful views of the 40-foot-high bluffs on the far side. After the trail crosses another footbridge, it runs along the bluff top, then, following a switchback descent, it travels along the bluff face close to the river. Along the way is a cavelike shelter made by roofing over a deep cleft in the rock. This south-facing shelter is a good place to build a warming fire and soak up some sun.

Directions at a glance

0.0 From the beach area bathhouse, go west between the road and the river, following brown-and-yellow trail signs.

0.1 Turn left (south), cross the footbridge and immediately turn right (west) onto the River Trail.

0.3 Cross County Highway Y and stay right (west) on the descending trail.

0.7 Turn right (north) and cross the footbridge.

0.8 Turn right (east) on the Bluff Trail as the Hardwood Trail goes left.

1.1 Continue straight (southeast) following the brown-and-yellow Trail Shelter and Scenic Overlook signs.

1.3 Cross County Highway Y and follow the Beach Trail to the trailhead.

As the trail climbs back up the bluff, you have some of the best views of the gorge. Using care, you can venture out onto some of the snow-covered rocks for a closer look or even a photo or two.

How to get there

From WI 52, 17 miles east of Wausau, turn south on County Highway Y. Go 1.5 miles and turn left at the brown-and-yellow sign: EAST UNIT, DELLS OF THE EAU CLAIRE SWIMMING BEACH. Follow the park road past the campground to the east end of the beach parking lot near the bathhouse.

Potawatomi State Park Black Trail
Sturgeon Bay, Wisconsin

Type of trail: ➤➤ ✦

Also used by: Snowmobiles cross the ski trails

Distance: 5.5 miles

Terrain: Flat to gently rolling, with one short, steep hill

Trail difficulty: Easy

Surface quality: Groomed, single tracked, skate lane

Food and facilities: Parking, an enclosed warming shelter with fireplace, a flowing well, and outdoor toilets are at the trailhead. Winter camping sites are available. A downhill ski/snowboarding hill is at the northwest corner of the park. All services are available in Sturgeon Bay, including ski retail, rental, and repair.

Fees: A daily or annual state park pass is required to enter the park by car. Pay at the park entrance visitor's booth or self pay station.

Events: Candlelight ski tour, second Saturday in February; Sturgeon Bay Winter Arts Festival, third weekend in February.

Phone numbers: Potawatomi State Park, (920) 746–2890; Door County Chamber of Commerce, (920) 743–4456.

Internet: www.doorcountyvacations.com

Across the channel from the trailhead warming shelter, Sturgeon Bay's shipyards lie frozen in winter's icy bond. You'll quickly ski past very different scenes. The deep forest of paper birch, maple, and pine has a primeval feel. Just west of the park is a site where the Potawatomi tribe withstood a long siege inside a fortified village in the early 1650s. Hundreds of Iroquois warriors had canoed from upstate New York to teach them a lesson for being too friendly with the French.

Kids love the trails at Potawatomi.

Potawatomi State Park Black Trail

Scale: 1:15,910 or 3.98" = 1 mile

Directions at a glance

0.0 From the trailhead shelter, go north on the groomed ski trail, following Hemlock Trail signs (small squares with hemlock branch silhouettes), blue-and-white skier silhouettes, and color-coded posts (green, blue, black, red). You will always follow the Black Trail. YOU ARE HERE map signs are at most intersections.

0.2 Ski around the steel gate and cross the park road. On the trail again, the Hemlock Trail splits off to the right. Turn left (south) following blue-and-white skier silhouette signs.

0.6 Turn right (north) at the top of a steep climb immediately after an intersecting trail goes downhill to the left.

1.8 Cross the park road and bear right as a short connector trail turns left. There is a YOU ARE HERE map sign at this intersection.

2.3 Turn left (west) as the Red Loop continues straight. There is a YOU ARE HERE map sign at this intersection.

3.4 Bear right (south) as a short connector trail turns left.

4.2 Turn right (south) as the Green Loop continues straight.

5.1 Continue straight (east) as the outbound, all colors trail turns left. Then make an immediate right turn (southeast) on a downhill trail.

5.2 Cross the park road and bear left (north). Follow to trailhead.

For the Potawatomi, winters were times for hunting, trapping, and gathering around the fire. They surely stalked game here, if the white-tailed deer were as plentiful as they are today. The warming shelter, with its stock of firewood, brings things back to basics, recalling a time when fire and a small enclosure meant survival in the long winter months.

The one-way counterclockwise ski begins with a short warm-up along the bay shore. Shipbuilding was the town of Sturgeon Bay's lifeblood when lake commerce thrived. Now, pleasure boats are the main marine craft manufactured there. The huge shipyards are the only ones on the Great Lakes large enough to handle giant thousand-foot freighters for repairs, so monstrous boats are often seen in the channel.

Turning inland the trail winds along a rocky bluff through cedars and paper birch for 0.3 mile before angling up the only steep climb of the route, about 50 feet in 0.1 mile. On top, skiing is easier, flat to gently rolling, through dense maple, oak, pine, and paper birch. Numerous loops split off and rejoin the Black Trail. There are another 3 miles of ski trail here. The Green and Red Loops are for classic ski striding only.

Snowshoers are directed to the half-mile Ancient Shores Nature Trail near the campground.

As you ski north then west, you are gradually climbing. You won't notice the slight grade that takes you to a point 130 feet above the trailhead. It will energize you on the return leg though. Easy double poling will be all that's needed to get you back. The last 50-foot drop down the bluff adds a bit of excitement near the end.

How to get there

From WI 42/5, 2 miles west of Sturgeon Bay, go north on Park Road for 2.5 miles to the Potawatomi State Park entrance on the right.

Peninsula State Park Minnehaha Trail

Fish Creek, Wisconsin

Type of trail:	⬤⬤⬤
Also used by:	Hikers
Distance:	2.4 miles round-trip
Terrain:	Flat
Trail difficulty:	Easy
Surface quality:	Ungroomed, snowshoer and hiker packed
Food and facilities:	Parking and outdoor toilets are at the trailhead. Indoor shelter, water, and toilets are at the park office at the entrance. Winter campsites are available; register at the park office. All services are available in Fish Creek, including lodging and dining at the exceptional White Gull Inn.
Fees:	A daily annual state park pass is required to enter the park by car. Pay at the park office at the park entrance.
Events:	Candlelight ski tour and Fish Creek Winter Games, first weekend in February.
Phone numbers:	Peninsula State Park, (920) 854–5791; Door County Chamber of Commerce, (920) 743–4456.
Internet:	www.doorcountyvacations.com

Scenic Peninsula State Park is quiet in winter. One of the state's most popular in summer, the solitude you'll find will be a relief from the crowds. This is also true for the village of Fish Creek. The quaint fishing port retains much of the nineteenth-century character it seems to lose when the streets are crowded with cars and tourists. The White Gull Inn

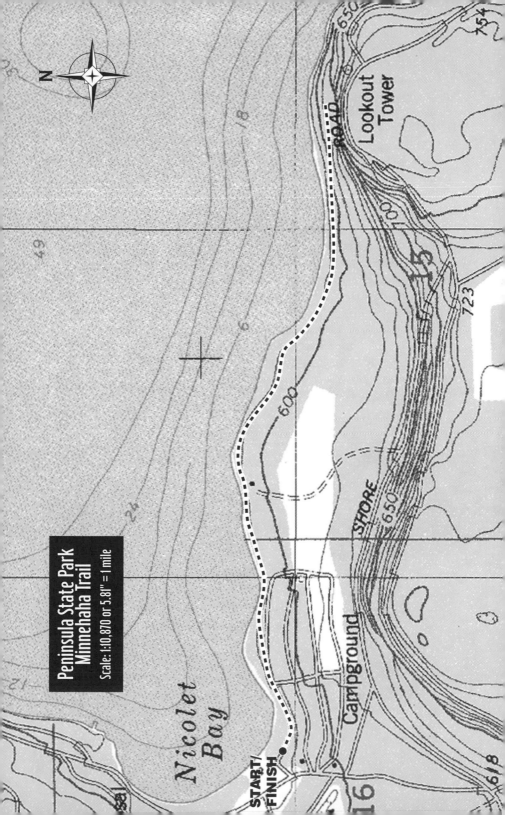

N

**Peninsula State Park
Minnehaha Trail**
Scale: 1:10,870 or 5.81" = 1 mile

Nicolet Bay

START/
FINISH

Campground

SHORE

ROAD

Lookout
Tower

15

16

754

723

618

49

24

12

18

6

600

650

650

100

650

700

serves breakfast, lunch, and dinner. The traditional Door County fish boil is basic, but delicious, fisherman's fare of whitefish, potatoes, and onions.

Peninsula Park is a peninsula on a peninsula. The Door County Peninsula is a long, narrow stratum of resistant dolomite limestone that split the advancing glacier into the Michigan and Green Bay lobes. The sheer bluff faces at Peninsula State Park taught scientists several things about postglacial times. Lake levels varied greatly as the glacier retreated. Caves washed by higher levels are found in the cliffs. The old shorelines are no longer horizontal, showing that the tremendous weight of the ice deformed the earth's crust. This depression formed an angle, with the hinge being in southern Wisconsin at the farthest extent of the ice. Door County is still rising about an inch every hundred years.

Directions at a glance

0.0 From the east side of the parking area, follow the trail near the shore to the east through a picnic area.

1.2 Turn around at the beginning of the Eagle Trail and return to the trailhead.

You will get a good look at the cliffs as you follow the trail to Eagle Bluff. There was no specific sign for the Minnehaha Trail at the trailhead when I visited. Still, it is easy to follow because it is the trail closest to the shore. The trail passes through beautiful stands of cedar and birch. In the distance to the north lies Horseshoe Island.

People often leave the trail for the open ice, where fantastic sculptures have been formed. Use extreme caution traveling on ice. Always take ski poles. If you fall through the ice, you can use them to pull yourself out by gripping each pole low near the basket and pounding the tips into the ice. Sound scary? It is.

How to get there

From WI 42 at the east end of the village of Fish Creek, turn north into Peninsula State Park. The park office is immediately on the left. Go north on Shore Road for 2.5 miles then turn right (east) on Bluff Road. Follow Bluff Road for 0.5 mile until it rejoins Shore Road. Turn left (west) on Shore Road, following signs to Nicolet Bay.

Frozen lake waves sculpt caves along the bay shore.

Bear Paw Inn Bear Paw Trail

White Lake, Wisconsin

Type of trail:	🟤
Distance:	3 miles
Terrain:	Rolling, with steep sections
Trail difficulty:	More difficult
Surface quality:	Ungroomed, snowshoer packed
Food and facilities:	Parking, indoor heated shelter and toilets, food and beverages, lodging, snowshoe rental, retail, and repair, and ski rental are at the trailhead. A tent warming shelter is near the halfway point. Some services are available in Langlade, 2.5 miles north. All services are available in Antigo, 22 miles west.
Events:	Snowshoe Torch Walks and Dinner, New Year's Eve and some Saturdays in January and February; Snowshoe Rendezvous races, second Saturday in January; Snowshoe Day Hike, third Sunday in January; Winterfest, second weekend in February.
Phone numbers:	Bear Paw Inn, (715) 882–3502; Antigo Area Chamber of Commerce, (715) 623–4134 or (888) 526–4523.
Internet:	www.newnorth.net/antigo.chamber (Antigo Area Chamber of Commerce); www.bearpawinn.comm (Bear Paw Inn).
Equipment note:	Traditional or modern snowshoes will do. Poles are recommended.

There is always something happening at the Bear Paw Inn. More than 230 classes, clinics, and workshops are presented here, on everything from white-water kayaking to snowshoe lacing, from home brewing to winter poetry writing, from cross-country skiing to fly-fishing. The Sun Bear Restaurant serves breakfast and lunch and, on weekends, dinner by reservation. The menu emphasizes made-from-scratch healthy eating. And you can get a good beer there too.

The rapid waters of the Wolf River are close by. A system of eight trails, all starting at the inn, serves skiers, snowshoers, hikers, and mountain bikers. The Nicolet National Forest is practically across the road and that all-important ingredient, snow, is abundant. There are 10 miles of cross-country ski trails, many groomed for skating as well as classic skiing. YOU ARE HERE map signs at nearly all intersections makes following ski or snowshoe trails easy.

Leaving the Trading Post and following the Bear Paw Trail in a counterclockwise direction, the trail quickly plunges into a dense forest of

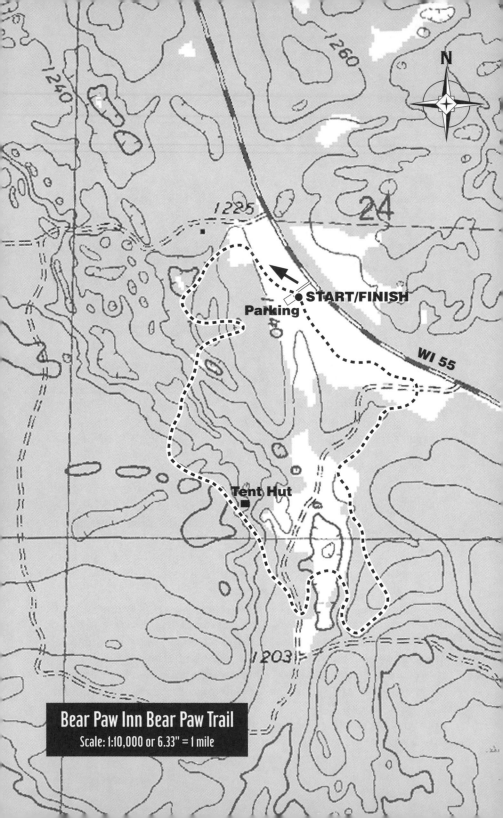

N

1240

1260

24

1225

START/FINISH

Parking

WI 55

Tent Hut

1203

Bear Paw Inn Bear Paw Trail
Scale: 1:10,000 or 6.33" = 1 mile

Directions at a glance

0.0 From the west side of the parking lot across from the Bear Paw Inn Trading Post, go west on the Bear Paw Loop.

0.9 Turn left (southeast) toward the Tent Hut as the Bear Paw Trail splits.

1.3 Cross the Black Bear ski trail.

2.2 Cross the Black Bear ski trail.

2.6 Cross the Panda ski trail twice. Continue to trailhead.

oak, maple, aspen, birch, and white pine. Fox and white-tailed deer are often seen. A bobcat footprint was spotted recently and there is a coyote den near the south end of the loop.

The trees close in on this narrow, twisty loop that serves as a demanding single track mountain bike trail in summer. Here and there in the forest you'll spot huge glacial boulders. Near the halfway point a canvas tent is stocked with firewood. You are welcome to build a fire in its woodstove.

Beyond the tent, you'll find more twisting through the dense forest until you cross the old road that serves as a wide ski trail—turn north at this point. Soon the trail breaks out into the open and swings east through a broad, tree-bare pit. Back in the woods again, the trail continues to snake around and climb for a short distance. Then, as you turn north a final time, the terrain becomes more moderate all the way back to the inn.

How to get there

From the town of Langlade, go southeast 2.5 miles on WI 55 to the Bear Paw Inn on the right.

The Trading Post outfits snowshoers and skiers.

Rib Lake Ice Age Trail

Rib Lake, Wisconsin

Type of trail:

Also used by:	Dogs and skijorers
Distance:	2.3 miles
Terrain:	Gently rolling
Trail difficulty:	Easy
Surface quality:	Groomed frequently, single tracked, skate lane
Food and facilities:	Parking and a newly built outdoor toilet are at the trailhead. All services are available in Rib Lake, 5 miles south, including lodging and good food at Camp 28 Resort Hotel. Trail Farms B&B is 4 miles northwest of the trailhead.
Events:	Hinder Binder cross-country ski race, third Saturday in February.
Phone numbers:	Rib Lake Commercial and Civic Club, (715) 427–5761 or (800) 819–5253; Ice Age Park and Trail Foundation, (800) 227–0046.

Want trails? Rib Lake's got them. Ski and snowshoe trails loop through the deep hemlock-laced forest. One trail runs right to the edge of town. The Timms Hill National Trail goes from the Ice Age Trail all the way to the state's highest point, a distance of 9 miles. In the summer, a section of the Ice Age Trail is wheelchair accessible.

Countless hours of activism and volunteerism have gone into creating the system. An amazing job for a community of fewer than a thousand people. The town's motto is "Where the Ice Age ends and your adventure begins." The glacial moraine is gentle here. Hills are in the 20- to 30-foot range—adventure doesn't require great expertise. Lots of trails and a small

Skiers stride the Ice Age Trail.

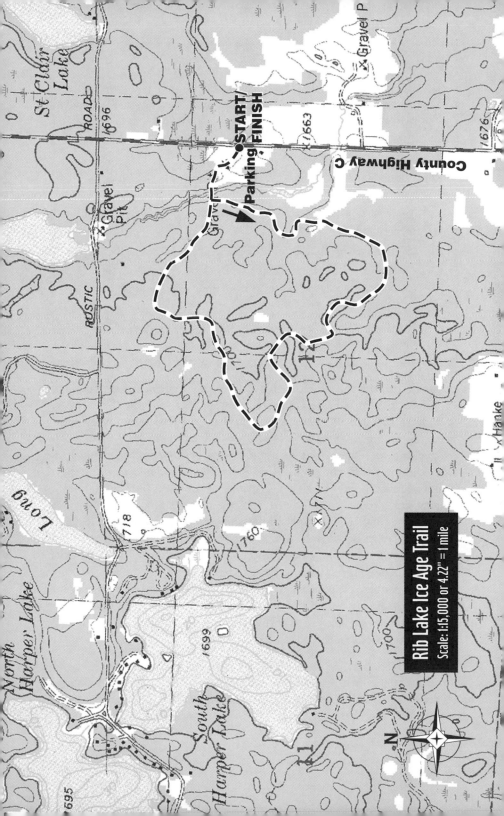

St Clair Lake

ROAD

1696

Gravel Pit

RUSTIC

●START/FINISH

Parking

County Highway C

1663

Gravel P

× Gravel P

1676

Long

718

1760

700

× 717

ft Hanke

North Harper Lake

1699

South Harper Lake

1695

Rib Lake Ice Age Trail
Scale: 1:15,000 or 4.22" = 1 mile

N

Directions at a glance

0.0 From the trailhead sign board, pass under the arch going west on the groomed ski trail following yellow, red, blue, and Ice Age Trail marked posts.

0.1 Turn left (south) on the Ice Age Trail (yellow) as the red and blue marked trail goes straight.

0.8 Continue straight (northwest) as the green Nordic Trail merges from the left.

1.1 Turn left (northwest) as the Promenade (blue beginner's trail) merges from the right.

1.3 Continue straight (west) on the blue marked trail as the Ice Age Trail turns left.

2.0 Continue straight (southeast) as the Timms Hill National Trail turns left.

2.2 Continue straight (east) as the Ice Age Trail turns right, and return to the trailhead.

population means you'll find much solitude. Trails here are never crowded.

The cross-state Ice Age Trail travels through a slice of lumberjack history north of Rib Lake. An easy clockwise loop on the two-way trails begins by taking you past the site of long-gone lumber Camp 6. An interpretive sign for Camp 6 shows a photo of a prize-winning load of logs from early in the twentieth century. A lumberjack stands atop the massive load, piled high on a sleigh. Portions of the trails here were once a logging sleigh route.

After looping to the south and around to the north on the Ice Age Trail, you'll junction with the Promenade, part of the beginner loop. Now the trail becomes more moderate, though no less scenic, as it tracks through the deep forest back to the trailhead.

Some people combine running a dog with cross-country skiing. A special dog harness, tether, and waist belt put dog power into skiing. This is the Scandinavian sport of skijoring. You might want to step out of the way if you see one of these teams coming.

How to get there

From WI 102, 2 miles east of the town of Rib Lake, go north on County Highway C for 2.7 miles to the Ice Age Trail parking lot on the left.

Timms Hill Park Green Trail

Ogema, Wisconsin

Type of trail:	▬ ◄ ▩
Distance:	2.9 miles (3.3 miles with snowshoe side trip to the Timms Hill observation tower)
Terrain:	Flat and hilly with steep sections
Trail difficulty:	Most difficult
Surface quality:	Groomed, single tracked, skate lane
Food and facilities:	Parking and lodging at the Catch A Dream Lodge. Open shelter and outdoor toilets at Timms Hill County Park. All services are available in Rib Lake, 14 miles south.
Events:	Timms Hill Trudge snowshoe race, first weekend in March.
Phone numbers:	Price County Tourism Department, (800) 269–4505 or (715) 339–4505; High Point Village, (715) 767–5287; Rib Lake Village Hall, (800) 819–LAKE.
Equipment note:	Modern or bear paw snowshoes are recommended for the side trip to the observation tower.

You may think 1,951 feet of elevation seems a bit threatening. That's the height of Timms Hill, the highest point in Wisconsin. What makes it an attainable adventure is that the hill's actual elevation above the level of Bass Lake is only 160 feet. You can get bragging rights for having been to the high point without too much strain.

It's easy to see what's ahead as you look north from the Catch a Dream Lodge. Across Bass Lake, fire and observation towers rise above thickly wooded Timms Hill. Everything seems so idyllic. There are no crowds, which is part of the appeal of staying at this beautiful little resort. Owners Lyle and Kathleen Blomberg

Snowshoing down from Wisconsin's highest hill.

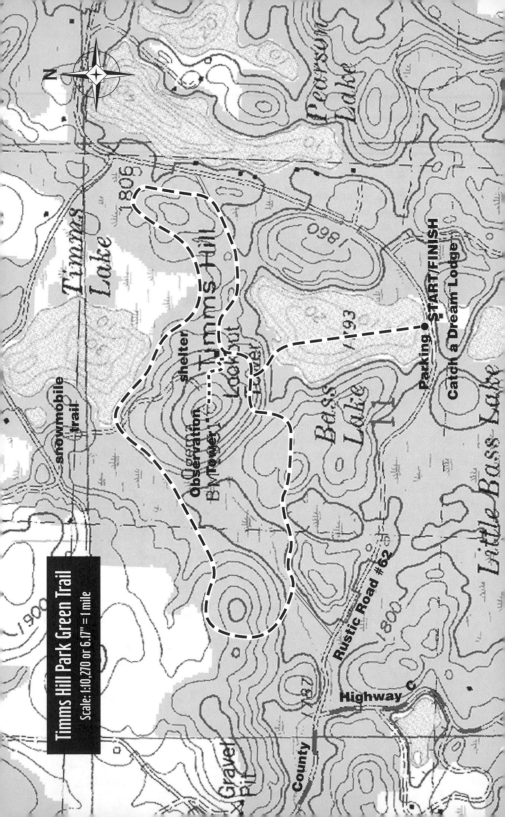

Timms Hill Park Green Trail
Scale: 1:10,270 or 6.17" = 1 mile

N

START/FINISH

Parking

Catch a Dream Lodge

Observation
B tower
shelter
Lookout

Timms Hill

Timms Lake

Pearson Lake

Bass Lake

Little Bass Lake

snowmobile
Trail

Highway C

Rustic Road #62

County

Gravel Pit

1800

1900

1805

860

793

787

Directions at a glance

0.0 From the north side of Rustic Road 62 at Catch A Dream Lodge, go north across Bass Lake on the groomed ski trail.

0.3 Turn left (west) at a "T" intersection. The trail now runs on the unplowed park road and is marked with green, blue, and red tree blazes. To complete the loop you will always follow green blazes.

0.5 Bear right (west) as the Ice Age Trail (red blazes) goes left.

0.8 Turn right (west) as the green marked trail leaves the road.

1.6 Continue straight across a snowmobile trail.

2.1 Turn right (south) as the access spur trail goes straight.

2.3 Turn right (west) onto the unplowed park road as the blue trail goes straight.

2.5 Turn left (south) at the open shelter, or, if on snowshoes, go straight for 0.2 mile up the trail to the observation tower at the top of Timms Hill and return.

2.6 Turn left (southeast) off of the park road and cross Bass Lake to the trailhead.

prize this pristine location. Lyle is descended from Swedish pioneers who first settled this area, and he did most of the lodge construction himself.

Quiet little Bass Lake is your warm-up stretch. Trail grooming is handled by the Highpoint Ski Club, which takes pride in keeping the trails in top shape. The clockwise one-way loop leaves Timms Hill for last. Timms is the big hill, but there is also a 100-foot climb waiting for you. One of Timms' buddies is hanging around the west end of the loop. A long gradual downhill run with a great view of Timms follows the climb.

If you are on snowshoes, a steep switchback trail runs up to the observation tower from a bronze marker near the park shelter. You can also visit it on skis if you are willing to ski up the snowmobile trail that goes from Timms Lake to the top. The view from the observation tower is fantastic. Bundle up; the wind always seems to blow up there.

How to get there

From WI 86, turn south on County Highway C. Travel 0.9 mile to Rustic Road 62 and turn left (east). Go 0.7 mile to the Catch a Dream Lodge.

Palmquist's The Farm Sugarbush Trail

Brantwood, Wisconsin

Type of trail:	▬ ⟨ 🔲
Also used by:	Skijorers and dogs
Distance:	3.2 miles
Terrain:	Flat
Trail difficulty:	Easy
Surface quality:	Groomed frequently, single tracked, skate lane
Food and facilities:	Parking, indoor heated shelter and toilets, ski and snowshoe rental, lodging, food, and beverages are at the trailhead. All services are available in Tomahawk, 21 miles east.
Fees:	A daily trail pass is charged.
Phone numbers:	Palmquist's The Farm, (715) 564–2558 or (800) 519–2558; Tomahawk Chamber of Commerce, (715) 453–5334 or (800) 569–2160.
E-mail:	tmhwkcoc@newnorth.net (Tomahawk Chamber of Commerce).

Farming can be a tough life anywhere. This is especially true around the forty-fifth parallel, halfway between the equator and the North Pole. Here, Palmquist's The Farm is in the transition zone, where farmland gives way to the vast Chequamegon Forest (SHA-wa-ma-gun). With hard work, settlers carved a life from this land. When they needed to get around in winter, they used skis. At The Farm, people have skied the trails for more than one hundred years. Jim Palmquist's father skied to school and courted Jim's mom on skis. Winter was a time for fun then and now at The Farm.

The Palmquist family—Helen, Jim, Art, Toinie, and Anna—have had a cross-country ski touring center at The Farm for nearly three decades. It is

still a working farm with cattle and horses. Guided ski tours let you roam with deer and buffalo. The hardy Belgian horses do their share by pulling guests through the woods on a big logging sleigh piled with comfy hay and blankets.

Comfort, fun, and great home cooking are highlights of a visit to Palmquist's. There are five lodging options, from the

Synchronized skiers glide along the Sugarbush Trail.

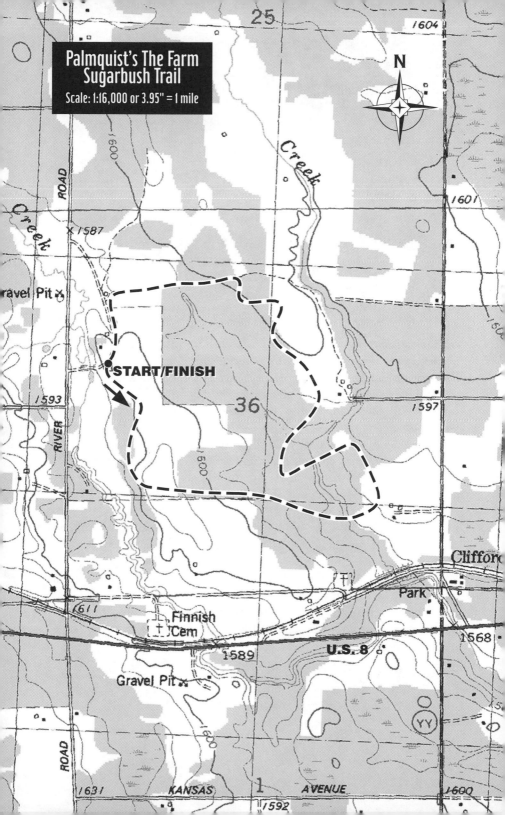

Directions at a glance

0.0 From the trailhead at the southwest corner of the barn, go southeast on the one-way groomed Sugarbush Trail. Stay left as a trail splits right.

0.1 Turn right (southwest).

0.4 Bear left (east) on the Sugarbush Trail at a four-way intersection.

0.8 Continue straight (east) on Alba's Trail as the Sugarbush Trail turns left.

2.0 Turn right (north) on the Sugarbush Trail.

2.5 Bear right (north) as the trail around Jack Lake goes left.

2.7 Turn left (west) on the Sugarbush Trail as the Gray Fox Trail goes straight.

3.1 Turn left (south) at a "T" intersection and follow to trailhead.

original farmhouse to cozy cabins, all with fireplaces or woodstoves. Meals made from scratch on a wood-burning stove reflect the Palmquist's Finnish heritage. Needless to say there is a sauna. Massage therapy is available by appointment. On Saturday nights The Farm livens up with folk music and stories, just like the days when people created their own entertainment.

Skiing doesn't have to be hard to be fun. Excellent grooming at The Farm ensures the best possible trail conditions for novice or expert skiers. Besides the Sugarbush Trail, there are another 10 miles of trails here. A short loop off of the Sugarbush Trail is lined with strings of white Christmas lights for night skiing.

Skiing counterclockwise on the mostly one-way Sugarbush Trail, you quickly leave the mooing cattle behind for the quiet fields and woods. Swinging east, the trail descends gradually into the little valley of Somo Creek and onto Alba's Trail, a drop of 40 feet. Looping up and down and over the creek several times, the trail climbs up into a stand of sugar maple trees—the sugarbush—where trees were tapped in spring to make syrup. It may set you dreaming of big stacks of pancakes at the farmhouse kitchen.

How to get there
From U.S. 8, 21 miles west of Tomahawk, go north on River Road for 1 mile to Palmquist's The Farm entrance drive on the right.

Minocqua Winter Park Nutcracker Trail

Minocqua, Wisconsin

Type of trail:	
Distance:	2.7 miles
Terrain:	Hilly with very steep sections
Trail difficulty:	Most difficult
Surface quality:	Groomed frequently, single tracked, skate lane
Food and facilities:	Parking, heated indoor shelter, food and beverages, waxing area, child care, ski lessons, ski retail, rental, and repair are available at the trailhead. All services are available in Minocqua/Woodruff. Check out the coffee, soups, and sandwiches at Hoorhay's on the main drag.
Fees:	A daily or annual trail pass is required.
Events:	Demo Days, free equipment demos, second weekend in December; Ski Fest, free lessons and demos, second Sunday in January; Howard Young Cup ski races, first Saturday in March.
Phone numbers:	Minocqua Winter Park, (715) 356–3309; Minocqua–Arbor Vitae–Woodruff Area Chamber of Commerce, (715) 356–5266 or (800) 446–6784.
Internet:	www.minocqua.org

Winter Park is one of Wisconsin's all-time favorite cross-country ski destinations. It is an ideal ski area for everyone from rank beginners to experts. Two dozen trails with 44 miles of distance are groomed to a T with state-of-the-art equipment. There are trail name signs and YOU ARE HERE maps at every intersection. With its comfortable Chalet, where you'll find food, drinks, a waxing room, child care, and a ski shop, Winter Park has the perfect balance between action and relaxation. Regularly scheduled professional skiing instruction has helped hundreds learn or improve.

This is an exiting place, where the love of cross-country

A skier skates away from the Chalet at Winter Park.

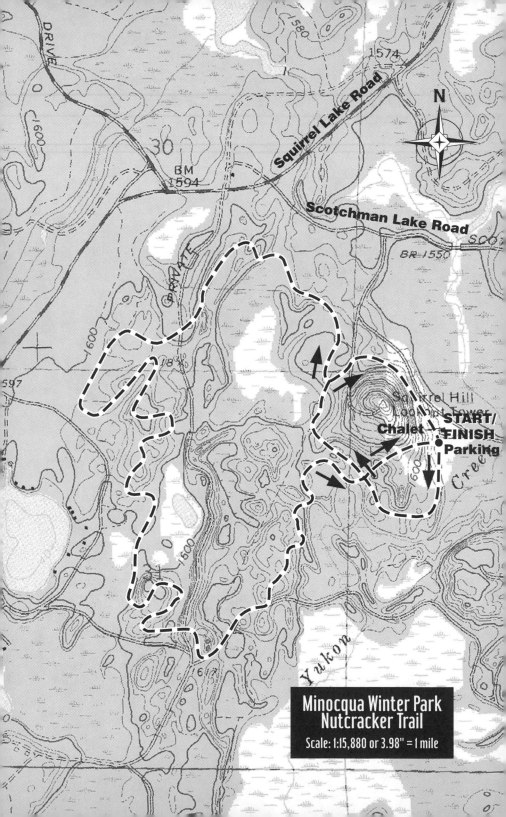

skiing is infectious. In the ski shop, Dan and Lona Clausen are always on top of the latest ski technology and are able to outfit skiers of all abilities. Kids have a great time here. The broad, open instruction area outside the Chalet is a perfect place for them to learn the fun of skiing on their own or in a group. Because of the growing popularity of snowshoeing, a trail has been designated especially for shoeing.

Everyone can improve their skills at Winter Park, thanks to the intertwining of trails of all levels of difficulty. Skiers can take on new challenges in bits and pieces. Winter Park has many wonderful trails, but one is legendary among accomplished skiers: the Nutcracker.

The Nutcracker takes advantage of every possible foot of elevation on steep glacial ridges. Exciting turns that some consider diabolical are mixed in. It is not a trail to ski in icy conditions unless you are a true expert. The groomers can turn ice into what they call "hero snow" that lets you ski fast with control. Speed is not always an asset on the Nutcracker.

Skiing south from the Chalet on the mostly one-way trail system, you get to warm up for 0.7 mile on the tame clockwise Base Loop and on Tornado Alley. Turning north on the counterclockwise Nutcracker, you start hitting the tough stuff. Though the relief on the hills is only 50 to 60 feet, the steepness and tricky turns produce 1.25 miles of intense skiing that seems much longer than it actually is.

The ridge tops afford fine overviews of the forest, thanks to a tornado that came through and flattened many trees. The fire tower on Squirrel Hill seems in a different quadrant every time you spot it as the Nutcracker twists around. Keep an eye out for wolf tracks. They have made a den nearby.

Directions at a glance

0.0   From the Chalet, ski south over a broad open area and pick up the Base Loop trail about 100 yards away as it enters the woods.

0.3   Continue straight (northwest) as the Beaver Pond Trail crosses.

0.4   Turn right (north) at a "T" intersection as Nose Dive Alley goes left.

0.5   Turn left (north) on Tornado Alley as the Base Loop continues straight.

0.7   Turn right (northwest) on the Nutcracker as Tornado Alley continues straight.

0.8   Bear right (southwest) on Nutcracker as Windy Ridge splits off left.

2.0   Turn left (northeast) on X-C Express at a "T" intersection.

2.2   Turn left (north) on Beaver Pond as X-C Express continues straight. Follow to trailhead.

When you finally leave Nutcracker you have an easy 0.25 mile to regain your composure before applying your skills to the Beaver Pond Trail. This last leg is not as difficult as Nutcracker, but it does keep you on your toes. A final push over the 80-foot-high shoulder of Squirrel Hill completes the trip.

Not sure the Nutcracker is for you? Try it the morning after a heavy snowfall. It's not only easier to control your skis in fresh snow, it's more fun to fall in.

How to get there

From Minocqua, go west on WI 70 for 7.7 miles. Turn left (south) on Squirrel Lake Road and go 5.8 miles. Turn left (east) on Scotchman's Lake Road for 0.4 mile, then right (south) on the Minocqua Winter Park drive. Follow to the Chalet parking lot.

Afterglow Lake Resort #1 Trail

Phelps, Wisconsin

Type of trail:	▬ ◀
Distance:	1.6 miles
Terrain:	Flat
Trail difficulty:	Easy
Surface quality:	Groomed frequently, single tracked, skate lane
Food and facilities:	Parking, indoor heated shelter and toilets, lodging, food, and beverages are at the trailhead. Most services are available in Phelps. All services are available in Eagle River, 17 miles southwest, including ski retail and repair.
Fees:	Donations suggested.
Phone numbers:	Afterglow Lake Resort, (715) 545–2560; Phelps Chamber of Commerce, (715) 545–3800.

They sell snow at Afterglow Lake. Lots of it. Ten feet is the annual average; a few years ago the total doubled that. Skiing by the first of December is assured and the season goes all the way through March. They sell family fun and relaxation here too. Pete and Gail Moline and their sons Scott and Michael give a youthful, active sports image to the traditional Northwoods resort. Afterglow has been in Pete's family for a half century and there have been ski trails on the land since 1965.

Afterglow's main lodge has a whirlpool, sauna, workout room, and a family playroom. All the cottages are on the lake and have fireplaces and

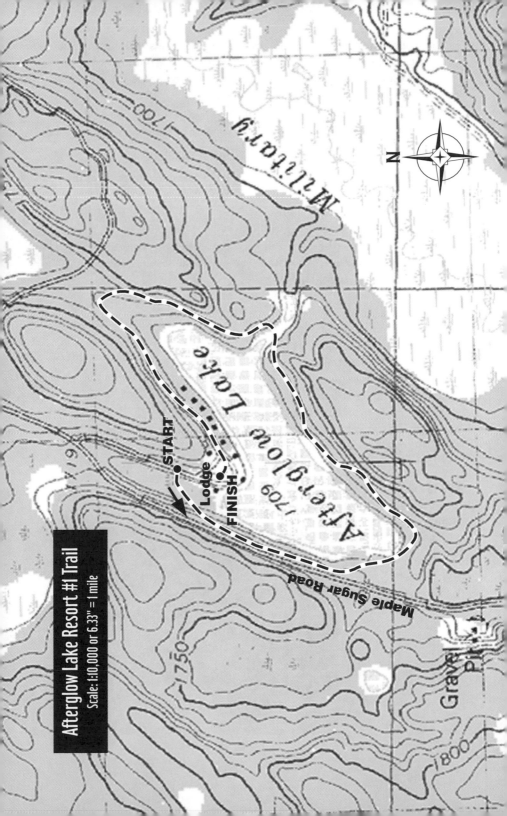

Afterglow Lake Resort #1 Trail

Scale: 1:10,000 or 6.33" = 1 mile

Military

Afterglow Lake

1709

START

Lodge

FINISH

Maple Sugar Road

Gravel Pit

1700

1750

1800

N

kitchens. For guests there is a hockey-size lighted ice skating rink and a 75-foot tubing hill across the lake. A roaring lakeside bonfire is kept up on weekends. There are lots of snowshoeing opportunities at the resort and in the adjacent Nicolet National Forest.

Trail #1 is a nice novice or family ski that tracks around the lake. Pete handles the trail grooming, something that he's a perfectionist at. In addition to #1 he grooms nine more trails with 10 additional miles of skiing on the property and in the national forest. The Phelps Trail is a classical-only loop that takes full advantage of 120 feet of elevation. Whatever trail you are on, you'll have much-prized solitude. Fewer than 400 skiers use the trails in a typical season.

Skiing counterclockwise from the lodge, two-way Trail #1 circles Afterglow Lake. The trail has a very intimate feel. Afterglow Lake is surrounded by forested hills with tall stands of spruce, balsam, hemlock, and birch. Fox are often seen and coyotes and fishers also live in the area. Deer often come by the lodge to feed. Stop in for coffee, hot chocolate, or cider after your ski—this is a good time to ask Pete what a fisher is.

Directions at a glance

0.0	From the west side of the parking area, go southwest on Trail #1, following green color-coded signs.
0.3	Continue straight (south) as Trail #9 turns right.
0.5	Turn left (northeast) as Trail #4 splits off to the right.
1.0	Turn left (northeast) as Trail #2 turns right.
1.3	Turn left (southwest) as Trail #5 splits off to the right. Follow to trailhead.

How to get there

From WI 17 in Phelps, go north on County Highway E for 1 mile. Turn right (east) on Maple Sugar Road and go 1.5 miles to the Afterglow Lake Resort entrance drive on the right.

Even sleds can get snowbound at Afterglow Lake Resort.

Red Cedar State Trail North

Menomonie, Wisconsin

Type of trail: ▬▬ ◄

Distance: 15.6 miles round-trip

Terrain: Flat

Trail difficulty: Easy

Surface quality: Groomed periodically, double tracked, skate lane

Food and facilities: Parking, and on weekends, heated indoor shelter, water, and indoor toilets are at the trailhead depot. All services are available in Menomonie, including ski retail and repair. Try the Silver Dollar Saloon for upscale bar food and good microbrews. Lourney and Jean's Tavern in Irvington serves generic pizza and sandwiches. In Downsville there are taverns, a country store, and the Creamery Restaurant and Inn, an outstanding place to stay and dine.

Fees: A daily or annual State Trail Pass is required to ski the trail. It can be purchased at the DNR office a short distance west of the trailhead on the north side of WI 29.

Events: Candlelight skiing, mid-January, in conjunction with Menomonie Winter Carnival.

Phone numbers: Menomonie Chamber of Commerce, (800) 283–1962 or (715) 235–9087; Wisconsin Department of Natural Resources, (715) 232–1242.

Tall timber built the city of Menomonie. Once home to Knapp, Stout & Company, the largest lumber mill in the world at the time, Menomonie prospered as huge stands of white pine were cut and floated down the Red Cedar River. Elegant homes are the city's hallmark. Stout's philanthropy, rare among lumber barons, endowed the college. The elegant Mabel Tainter Theatre was a memorial to a lumberman's daughter. It is open daily for tours.

Menomonie may be a small city, but it is a city nonetheless. You will be amazed at how quickly you can escape it on the Red Cedar State Trail. The abandoned railroad grade runs within sight of its namesake river for most of the distance to Downsville. It is a fast flowing river that freezes only in the coldest part of winter. You'll have a good chance at spotting a bald eagle soaring above open water, hoping to swoop down and clutch an unwary fish.

Between Menomonie and Irvington the two-way trail skirts rock faces dressed in frozen waterfalls from dripping meltwater.

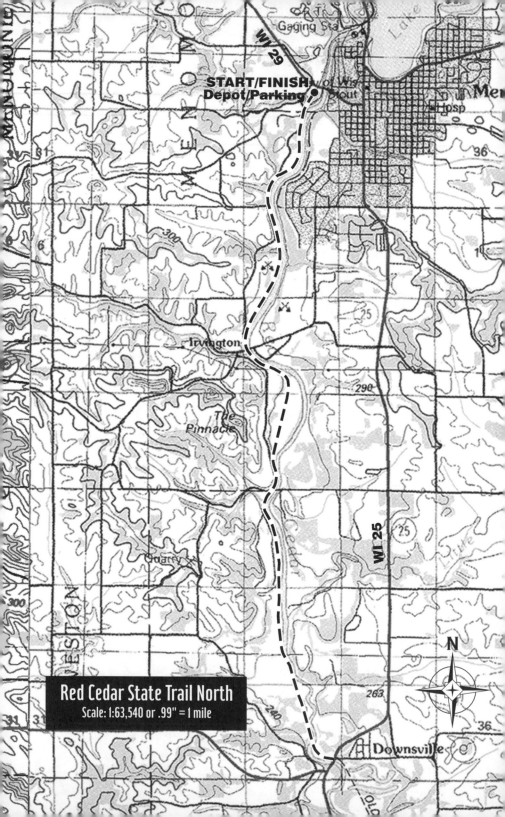

START/FINISH
Depot/Parking

WI 29

Gaging Sta

Lake

Men

Hosp

300

25

Irvington

290

The
Pinnacle

WI 25

25

Quarry

300

Cedar River

263

240

Red Cedar State Trail North
Scale: 1:63,540 or .99" = 1 mile

Downsville

OLD

N

South of Irvington, the trail strays from the river course and crosses a broad open area. Look to the west and see if you can spot any eagles or eagle nests in the treetops beyond the field. Returning to the river's edge, the trail again runs near the bluff slopes before crossing a beautiful stressed iron bridge just before Downsville.

Downsville seems like a metropolis compared to Irvington. It has two taverns, a country grocery, and a post office (cards postmarked Downsville are always a hit). T.J.'s Tavern serves a good Friday night fish fry and the Country Zone has great pizza. The place that you will write home about is the Creamery. Located on the east end of town on County Highway C, it has elegant lodging and a wonderful lunch and dinner menu. Fit for a lumberjack perhaps?

Directions at a glance

0.0 From the Red Cedar State Trail Depot, head south on the groomed ski trail.

3.0 Continue straight (south) underpassing the bridge in Irvington.

7.8 Turn around at Downsville and return to the trailhead.

How to get there

From I–94, take WI 25 south into Menomonie and turn right (west) on WI 29 (Eleventh Avenue). The trailhead depot is 0.4 mile on the left.

Watch for bald eagles over open spots on the Red Cedar River.

Red Cedar State Trail South

Downsville, Wisconsin

Type of trail:	▬▬▬▬ ▧
Also used by:	Hikers, skiers
Distance:	5.4 miles round-trip
Terrain:	Flat
Trail difficulty:	Easy
Surface quality:	Mechanically packed
Fees:	No fees for skiing or snowshoeing on the trail south of Downsville. See page 129 for fees required to ski on the machine-tracked trail to the north.
Food and facilities:	See "Food and facilities" on page 129.
Phone numbers:	Menomonie Chamber of Commerce, (800) 283–1962 or (715) 235–9087; Wisconsin Department of Natural Resources, (715) 232–1242.

Lumbering is a boom and bust business. Sleepy little Downsville seems little changed since the days when it thrived as a way point for rafters floating great quantities of rough sawn timber down to the Chippewa River. You have to wonder if the town could have held on today without the business brought in by the trail.

On the trail south of town, skis or snowshoes are your ticket to beautiful, tranquil rambling along the meandering Red Cedar River. The trail is maintained for hiking and snowshoeing by the ski trail groomer, which packs it down after a heavy snow. No ski tracks are set, so you'll make your own unless others have skied it first.

The first 2 miles of your journey takes you away from the river through flat bottomland. This offers a nice perspective of the river bluffs in the distance. It is a good place to catch a glimpse of a soaring red-tailed hawk on the lookout for small rodents.

Your destination is a big bend in the trail and river where waterfalls stand in frozen wonder on the steep stone bluffs. The trail is sandwiched between the rock face and the broad

Directions at a glance

0.0 From the trail rest area on the south side of the bridge at Downsville, head south on the packed trail.

2.7 Turn around at mile marker 11 and return to Downsville.

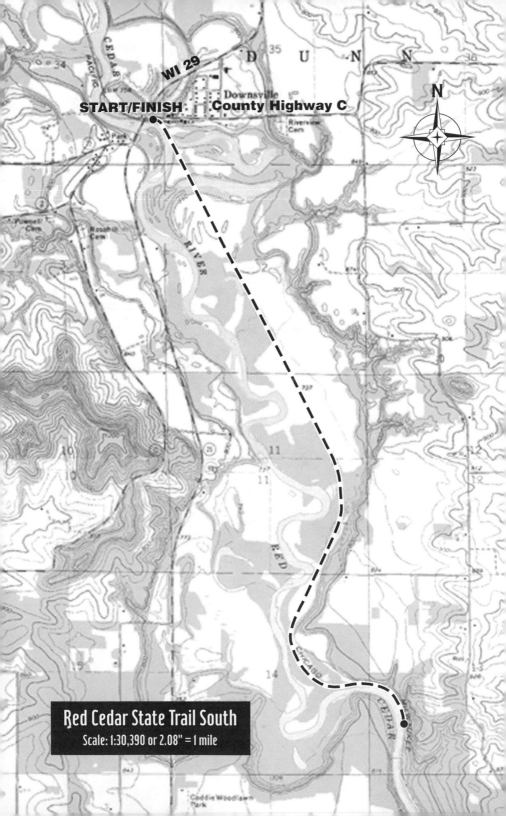

START/FINISH

WI 29

Downsville
County Highway C

N

Red Cedar State Trail South
Scale: 1:30,390 or 2.08" = 1 mile

curve of the river. A striking contrast between water in motion and water arrested.

If you are very ambitious, you can keep heading south to County Highway Y, another 1.25 miles farther on. The trail isn't groomed in this section. At County Highway Y you will be at the site of a genuine ghost town. Dunnville was once a thriving steamboat port in the lumbering heyday. It was the county seat too. Now there isn't even a wood chip to remind you of its past glory.

How to get there

From I–94, take WI 25 south for 11 miles through Menomonie to County Highway C in Downsville. Turn left (east) on County Highway C and make an immediate right turn (south) into the parking lot for the Red Cedar Trail.

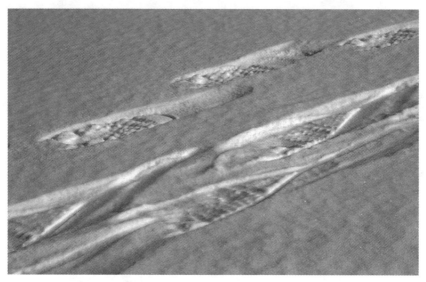

Tell-tale tracks in pristine new snow.

Interstate State Park Summit Rock/Echo Canyon Trails

St. Croix Falls, Wisconsin

Type of trail:	⬤
Also used by:	Hikers
Distance:	0.7 mile
Terrain:	Hilly with very steep sections
Trail difficulty:	Most difficult
Surface quality:	Ungroomed, snowshoer and hiker packed
Food and facilities:	Parking, open shelter, and outdoor toilets are at the trailhead. Indoor heated shelter and toilets are at the Ice Age Interpretive Center. All services are available in St. Croix Falls, 1 mile north.
Fees:	A daily or annual state park pass is required to enter via car. Pay at the Ice Age Interpretive Center or the self-pay station there.
Phone numbers:	Interstate State Park, (715) 483–3747; Polk County Information Center, (715) 483–1410 or (800) 222–POLK.
Equipment note:	Modern snowshoes and a ski pole are necessities.

The Summit Rock and Echo Canyon Trails pack a lot of gorgeous scenery into a very short loop. That doesn't mean it won't be difficult, only that it will be worth the effort. Interstate is one of the most stunning and geologically significant parks in the state. It was here that torrents of backed-up glacial meltwater met a wall of tough volcanic basalt. The mayhem that followed carved the Dalles, the deep river gorge framed by 80-foot cliffs. You will scale one of them. Summit Rock is the highest point on the bluffs, and the view of the gorge is grand.

The Ice Age Interpretive Center is a good place to get a short course on the wonders of the park and its native flora

The frozen St. Croix River passes between cliffs of volcanic rock.

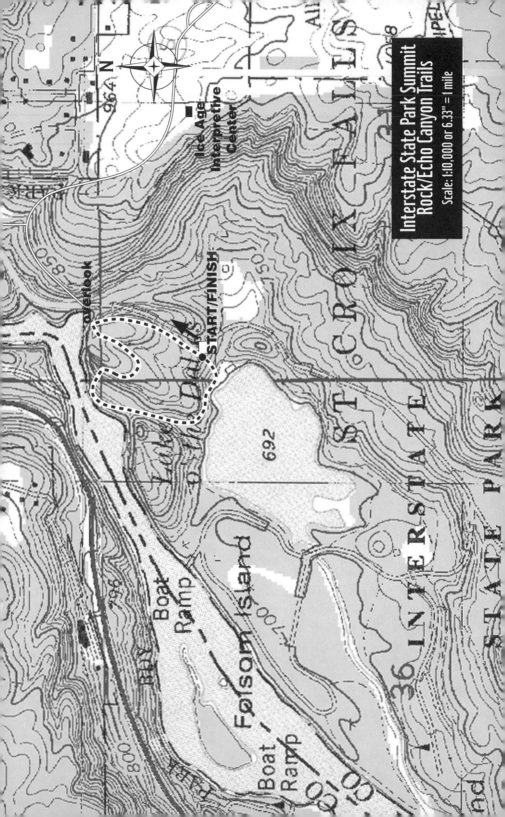

Interstate State Park Summit
Rock/Echo Canyon Trails

Scale: 1:10,000 or 6.33" = 1 mile

N

964

ST. CROIX FALLS

Ice Age
Interpretive
Center

Overlook

850

START/FINISH

50

692

ST. CROIX

Lake o'the Dalles

796

RIVER

Boat
Ramp

Folsom Island

Boat
Ramp

800

INTERSTATE

36 INTERSTATE STATE PARK

STATE PARK

and fauna. Among the park's fascinating phenomena are the potholes. As the raging water churned through the gorge, some rocks became trapped in whirlpools. Spinning around and around, they bored holes in the rock. The ones found in the park are between 5 and 25 feet in diameter and as deep as 80 feet.

Summit Rock and Echo Canyon are hiking trails with a number of short sections of stone steps and even one set of wooden steps. Modern snowshoes with crampons and ski poles are a must, as some sidestepping will be necessary. The wooden steps up to the Summit Rock overlook can even be climbed without taking the snowshoes off if there is a good amount of snow. This is probably safer than trying to climb slippery stairs while carrying the snowshoes. Using a ski pole and holding the railing with the other hand, you'll make it just fine.

From Summit Rock it's pretty much all downhill. There is more natural beauty in store as you wind down into Echo Canyon. This wonderful little gorge is lined with towering rocks. Also carved by glacial torrents, it is an intimate contrast to the Dalles.

An annual candlelight ski and snowshoe trek is held at the Ice Age Center the second Saturday in February. The trail used will be much easier. Candles or no candles, you wouldn't want to snowshoe to Summit Rock at night.

Directions at a glance

0.0   From the trailhead, go north on the Summit Rock Trail, climbing steeply and following brown-and-white arrows and hiker silhouette signs. YOU ARE HERE map signs are at intersections.

0.05 Stay right (north) as the Echo Canyon Trail goes left.

0.3   Turn right (west) on the Echo Canyon Trail, which joins on the left.

0.6   Turn left (east) on the Lake O' the Dalles Trail and follow to the trailhead.

How to get there

From the intersection of WI 35 and U.S. 8 in St. Croix Falls, go south on WI 35 for 0.5 mile and turn right into the Interstate State Park entrance road. Follow the road 1 mile to the small parking area on the left. If you pass the Lake O' the Dalles bathhouse, you have gone too far.

Interstate State Park Quarry Trail
St. Croix Falls, Wisconsin

Type of trail:	▬▬▬
Distance:	2 miles
Terrain:	Mostly flat with one steep uphill and downhill
Trail difficulty:	More difficult
Surface quality:	Groomed, single tracked
Food and facilities:	Indoor heated shelter and toilets are at the Ice Age Interpretive Center. All services are available in St. Croix Falls, 1 mile north.
Fees:	A daily or annual state park pass is required to enter via car. Pay at the Ice Age Interpretive Center or the self-pay station there.
Phone numbers:	Interstate State Park, (715) 483–3747; Polk County Information Center, (715) 483–1410 or (800) 222–POLK.

The Quarry Trail shows the kinder, gentler side of Interstate State Park. Until the last 0.1 mile, that is. It's there the trail earns its more difficult rating. Before that, the trail is a piece of cake; flat, with some great views across the frozen St. Croix River to the high bluffs on the Minnesota shore. Even the 100-foot climb up to the abandoned quarry is made on the gentlest slope possible.

From the South Campground the narrow, one-way, counterclockwise loop plunges into a beautiful mix of spreading, bare-branched oaks and tall, straight white pines. Oaks rely on strong winds to bring their leaves down; these wax-grabbing leaves may blow into the tracks anytime. Fresh snow is always appreciated.

Directions at a glance

0.0   From the South Campground parking lot, go north on the groomed single track trail, following white signs with black arrows. There are YOU ARE HERE map signs at most intersections. *Alternate route:* Turn right onto the Point Trail and follow it until it rejoins the Quarry Trail. This adds 2.1 miles to the tour.

0.8   Turn left (east) after crossing a stream as the Point Trail goes right.

1.9   Bear left on Lazy Run and be ready for a steep downhill. Follow to trailhead.

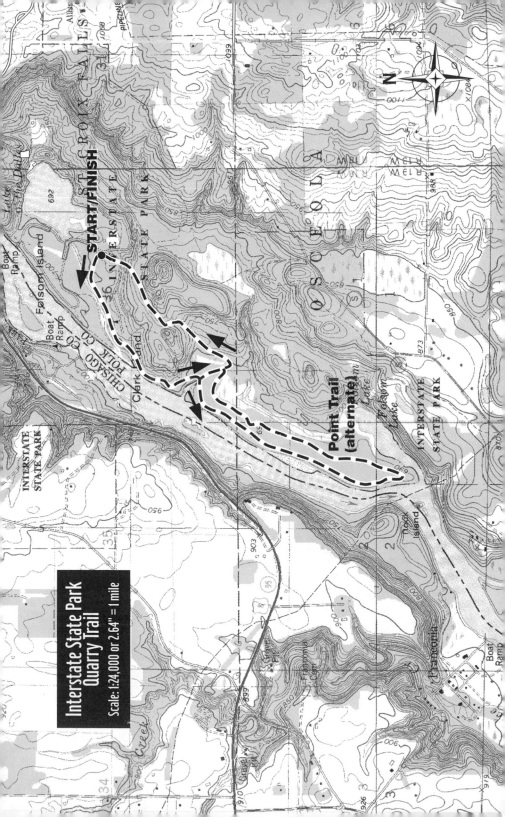

START/FINISH

INTERSTATE STATE PARK

CHISAGO CO. POLK CO.

Clark Island

Point Trail (alternate)

Folsom Lake

INTERSTATE STATE PARK

INTERSTATE STATE PARK

Boat Ramp

Boat Ramp

Folsom Island

Lake O'The Dalls

Nook Island

Boat Ramp

N

**Interstate State Park
Quarry Trail**

Scale: 1:24,000 or 2.64" = 1 mile

Breaking out of the woods, the trail runs along the edge of the St. Croix for 0.25 mile. Late in the winter you may see broken slabs of ice grinding against each other as eagles eye the open spots, looking for fish. Turning inland and crossing a small stream, you pass the turnoff for the Point Trail. This is a flat, easy loop that adds a little over 2 miles if you choose to try it. There are five other groomed trails in the park totaling 7 more miles of skiing.

On your way up the climb to the quarry, the Bluff Trail splits off to the right. This is the toughest trail in the park and should only be skied in good fresh snow conditions. I can say the same for the last leg of the Quarry Trail down Lazy Run. The ability to control speed by maintaining a good, wide snowplow is essential.

When I skied the long climb to the quarry, I saw signs of what might be called "a miracle of skiing." Someone, skiing down, was out of control and ran off the trail. My eyes followed the deviating tracks as they went through the deep snow straight for a tree. Then, just before the ultimate point of skier/tree contact, the tracks turned and cut back to the trail. Someone up above must look out for cross-country skiers. Don't assume you've lived a pure enough life to be so charmed. Snowplow and ski in control.

How to get there

From the intersection of WI 35 and U.S. 8, go south on WI 35 for 0.5 mile and turn right into the Interstate State Park entrance road. Follow the road 1.8 miles to the South Campground parking area on the left.

The woods open up around an abandoned quarry.

Sawyer County Forest Seeley Hills Advanced Trail

Seeley, Wisconsin

Type of trail: ➤➤ ◄

Also used by: Dogs

Distance: 3.2 miles

Terrain: Rolling, with some steep sections

Trail difficulty: More difficult

Surface quality: Groomed regularly, single tracked, skate lane

Food and facilities: Parking at the trailhead. Food in Seeley at the not-to-be-missed Sawmill Saloon. All services, including ski rental, retail, and repair, are available in Hayward, 11 miles south on U.S. 63. Hayward has numerous motels, hotels, resorts, and bed and breakfasts. The Angler's Bar and Coop's Pizza are noted for outstanding food and stuffed animals. For stuffed fish, stop in the Moccasin Bar to see the World Record Musky—a prime photo op.

Phone numbers: Hayward Area Chamber of Commerce, (800) 724–2992 or (715) 634–8662; Sawmill Saloon, (715) 634–5660.

The kingdom of Seeley, once just a wide spot in the road, is now a wide and high spot thanks to the gingerbread clock tower that rises above the Sawmill Saloon. You can survey it all from the overlook off of the Seeley Hills Advanced Trail. You may also spot gingerbread cottages sprinkled through the woods below. All this is the handiwork of local builder Gary Penman who, when asked after a few beers what he wanted to be when he grew up, answered, "I want to be the King of Seeley."

Seeley has become a haven for cross-country skiers looking for a quiet retreat in the forest. The main attraction is the American Birkebeiner trail (see page 144), 3 miles from town. The "Birkie" is the largest ski marathon in North America and one of the toughest in the world.

The Seeley Hills Trails are a new

A skier takes his dogs for a run on the Seeley Hills Trails.

Sawyer County Forest
Seeley Hills Advanced Trail
Scale: 1:13,330 or 4.76" = 1 mile

START/FINISH

County Highway OO

UHRENHOLDT MEMORIAL STATE FOREST

Old OO

1300

1400

1400

Seeley
(BM 1271)

overlook

Riverside Cem

CHICAGO

U.S. 63

AND

ST. CROIX NAT'L SCENIC RIVERWAY

NAMEKAGON R.

Sandpit

1307

1280

N

addition to the forest. Signage may vary as it becomes more formalized and permanent. The trail is toward the upper end of the more difficult rating. It could get dicey if conditions are icy. Otherwise the downhill runs are fairly gradual, with the steep stuff left for a few climbs. Total elevation change is 150 feet and the longest climb is 100 feet. Locals love to run their dogs when they ski. You are likely to see as many hounds as skiers.

From the trailhead you will roll over a heavily forested plateau, circling the loop in a counterclockwise direction. Just after turning north at the 1-mile point you'll be treated to a 0.3 mile downhill run through a narrow valley lined with birch and pine trees. A right turn at the bottom starts you on the longest, steepest climb of the loop.

Once back on top you can take a short side loop to the overlook of Seeley. In front of the town you'll see a beautiful stand of white pines. This is the Uhrenholdt Memorial Forest, where these trees will be left to grow to their true majesty. It's a fine place for a short snowshoe. There you'll be in tune with renowned author and snowshoer Sigurd Olsen, who wrote *The Singing Wilderness* and was instrumental in preserving the Boundary Waters Canoe Area in Minnesota. Olsen married into the Uhrenholdt family.

From the overlook, you'll work your way up a ridge and skirt the high point before a great, long downhill run to complete the loop. There are 5 more miles of trails in the Seeley Hills system along with a connector trail that can take you all the way to the Birkebeiner Trail (see page 144).

Directions at a glance

0.0   From the trailhead parking lot go around the steel gate and begin skiing southwest on the two-way groomed trail.

0.2   Turn left (south) as a trail signed DO NOT ENTER merges from the right.

0.7   Turn right (west) at a "T" intersection. The Easy Trail goes to the left.

1.0   Turn right (north) onto the Advanced Trail. The Easy Trail comes in from straight ahead and is marked DO NOT ENTER.

1.4   Turn right (east) onto the Advanced Trail. The trail straight ahead is signed DO NOT ENTER and goes onto private land.

1.9   Turn left (north) onto the trail to the Seeley overlook.

2.0   Bear left at a "Y" intersection, where you will follow a short loop trail down to the Seeley overlook.

2.2   Bear left as the trail rejoins the outbound leg.

2.3   Turn left (east) at a "T" intersection to rejoin the Advanced Trail.

3.0   Bear left onto the spur trail to the parking lot.

How to get there

From U.S. 63 at Seeley, turn east on County Highway OO (green-and-white signs say UHRENHOLDT FOREST AND SAWYER COUNTY SKIING AND HIKING TRAIL). After 0.3 mile, turn right (south) on Old "O" Road. At 1.2 miles, turn right into the small Seeley Hills Ski Trail parking area.

American Birkebeiner Trail
Cable, Wisconsin

Type of trail:

Also used by: All or part of the trail is the venue for several cross-country ski races.

Distance: 24.2 miles one-way

Terrain: Hilly with very steep sections

Trail difficulty: Most difficult

Surface quality: Groomed regularly, double tracked, wide skate lane

Food and facilities: Parking, a new enclosed shelter with a wood-stocked fireplace and a new outdoor toilet are at the north end. Parking, heated enclosed shelter, and outdoor toilets are at the midpoint (11 miles) at the County Highway OO road crossing. Parking, a new enclosed shelter with a wood-stocked fireplace, and a new outdoor toilet are at the south end off of Fish Hatchery Road. All services are available in Cable near the north end and Hayward near the south end. For food, check out the Angler's Bar and Coop's Pizza in Hayward and Nadine's Bistro in Cable. Ski rental, retail, and repair are in Hayward. In Seeley, 3 miles west of the trail at County Highway OO and U.S. 63, good soups, pizza, and grill food are at the Sawmill Saloon.

Fees: No mandatory fees at the north end; there is a donation box. A daily or annual parking fee is charged at the mid- and southern access parking lots.

Events: Seeley Hills Classic, last Saturday in January; Hayward Lions Pre-Birkie, second Saturday in February; American Birkebeiner Ski Marathon, last Saturday in February.

Phone numbers: Cable Area Chamber of Commerce, (800) 533–7454; Hayward Area Chamber of Commerce, (800) 724–2992 or (715) 634–8662; American Birkebeiner Ski Foundation, (715) 634–5025.

Internet: www.norwiski.com

The Birkebeiner is one big, wide, tough trail. One day a year this roomy, two-way trail through the pristine northwoods becomes very crowded and most definitely one-way. In late February about 7,000 skiers take to the trail in a test of speed, skill, and endurance called the American Birkebeiner.

Your visit is sure to be much less crowded, but no less tough. Obviously, you have the choice of doing an out-and-back ski of what ever length you choose. And, even if you work things to ski point-to-point, you won't have to ski as far as the Birkebeiner racers. Three miles are pared off the north end where the race starts adjacent to the Cable Airport; the south end trailhead is 4 miles short of the finish, across Lake Hayward on the town's Main Street. Hundreds of truckloads of snow are dumped on the pavement to ensure that skiers can get their finishing award medal and a beer within a minimal amount of time.

The tough part of the Birkie Trail is the hills. There's no getting around them. If you skied the whole way you'd have climbed 0.5 mile. While there isn't a single uphill that is more than a 150 feet, the hits just keep coming. The terrain is interlobate moraine or kettle moraine. The lobes of the Superior and Chippewa ice sheets ground against each other here, making the topography as pitted as the moon.

That said, you'll be surprised at how many recreational skiers take on the trail's challenge. There's never a dull moment and, anytime other than race day, there's plenty of room to maneuver on the downhills. The trail is about four times as wide as a typical trail. The American Birkebeiner Ski Foundation, which conducts the race, does a terrific job of grooming the trail.

From the north end trailhead, you'll climb for 4.8 miles to the trail's high point. This is near the site of the long-gone Seeley Fire Tower. You are skiing up and down nearly constantly, but each up is longer than the following down. Many skiers like to hit the

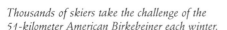
Thousands of skiers take the challenge of the 51-kilometer American Birkebeiner each winter.

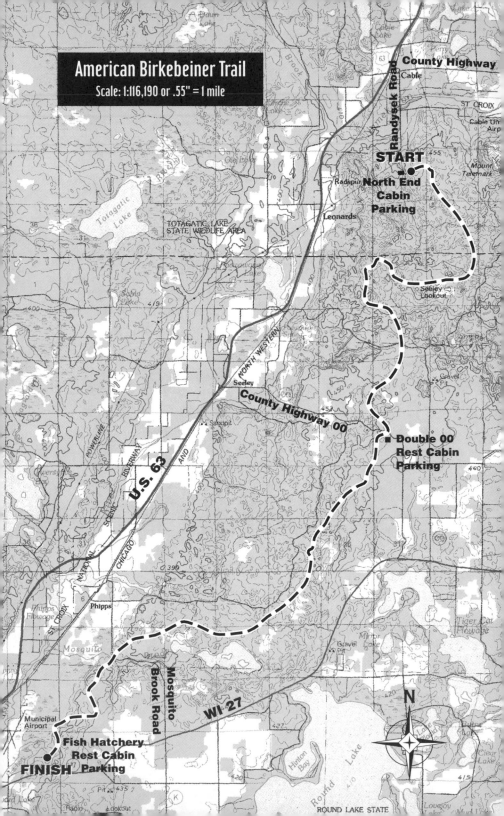

Directions at a glance

0.0 Follow the right ski trail uphill heading northeast (the other trail is marked DO NOT ENTER).

0.3 Turn right onto the Birkebeiner Trail. Ski out and back as far as you like or arrange transportation and ski one-way. Good turn-around points are the trail high point at 4.9 miles (9.8 miles round-trip), the midpoint at 11 miles where County Highway OO crosses (22 miles round-trip), or Mosquito Brook Road at 20.6 miles (41.2 miles round-trip).

high point, where there is an elevation marker, then turn around for a more down than up return.

Skiing the 11 miles to the midpoint shelter is also popular, especially if you stash some goodies there ahead of time. Go all the way and maybe you're ready to join the ranks of the Birkebeiner racers. Or do them one better and ski all the way to Mosquito Brook Road and back for a whopping 41.6 miles!

How to get there

From U.S. 63 in Cable, turn east on County Highway M for 0.2 mile. Look for a brown-and-white sign, AMERICAN BIRKEBEINER NORTH END TRAILHEAD 2 MILES, across from the Forest Lodge Library/Cable Natural History Museum and turn right (south) on Randysek Road (no sign). Travel 2 miles to the North End Trailhead parking area on the left (east) side of the road.

Bayfield County Forest North End B Trail

Cable, Wisconsin

Type of trail:	🐾
Also used by:	Cross-country skiers use the groomed ski trail you will be on for a short distance at the beginning and end. Stay well to the side and don't shoe on the ski tracks.
Distance:	3 miles
Terrain:	Rolling, with some steep sections
Trail difficulty:	More difficult
Surface quality:	Ungroomed, snowshoer packed
Food and facilities:	Parking, a new enclosed shelter with a wood-stocked fireplace, and a new outdoor toilet are at the trailhead. All services are available in Cable. Ski rental, retail, and repair are in Hayward, 17 miles south. For food, check out Nadine's Bistro in Cable, or the Sawmill Saloon in Seeley, 7 miles south.
Fees:	No mandatory fee, donation box.
Phone numbers:	Cable Area Chamber of Commerce, (800) 533–7454; Hayward Area Chamber of Commerce, (800) 724–2992 or (715) 634–8662; American Birkebeiner Ski Foundation, (715) 634–5025.
Internet:	www.norwiski.com

There are lots of great things you can say about the North End Trails: How local people organized to build the cozy cabin shelter with the fieldstone fireplace. How this finally gives a decent access point to the famed Birkebeiner Ski Trail (see page 144). How the idea of signing snowshoe loops of various distances has been a tremendous success.

Top accolades, however, have to go to the oversize outdoor toilet at the trailhead. It is big enough to be snowshoe friendly. And the fuzzy kittens thermometer near the door is a priceless touch.

Once on the trail you'll appreciate more than just the wonderful Northwoods

Any type of snowshoe is fine on the wooded North End Trails.

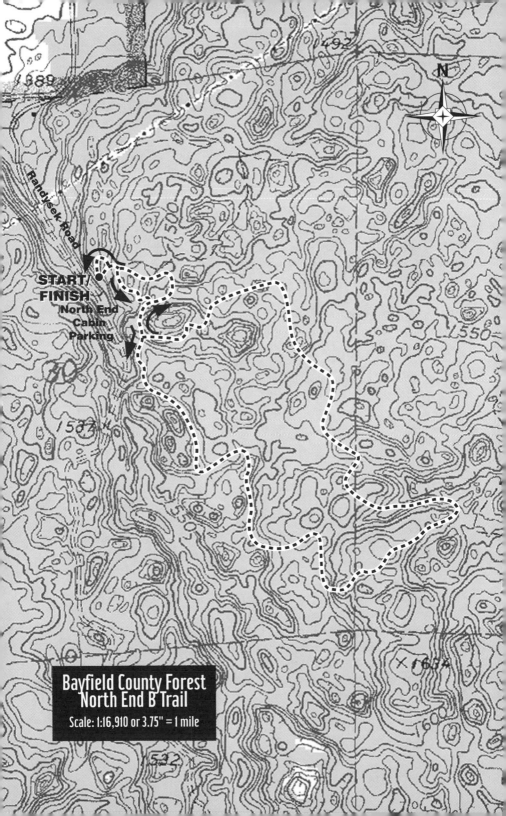

START/ FINISH

North End Cabin Parking

Raludysek Road

N

**Bayfield County Forest
North End B Trail**

Scale: 1:16,910 or 3.75" = 1 mile

scenery. Bright snowshoe silhouette cards and YOU ARE HERE maps at intersections let you enjoy the woods with confidence. The area is laced with old logging roads, some of which are used for the trail system. It would be very easy to get lost here. Local people, who know the area well, often set off on their own. A smart visitor will stick to the marked trail.

From the cabin shelter, your first leg will be a short climb on the groomed ski trail. A sharp right will take you onto the snowshoe-only trail. Now the trail is signed for one-way travel in a counterclockwise direction until you have completed the long loop. Leaving the ski trail, you'll keep climbing and, after you think you must be far from the cabin, you'll see it off to the right about 70 feet below. You'll have worked back around on a glacial ridge, a nice photo opportunity to show friends how ambitious you are. This will be just the start of your twisty, rolling journey.

At the south end of the long loop, the route circuits a beautiful, long, east-west ridge covered with white pine, paper birch, and oak trees. Look for scrolls of birch bark on the snow. Strong winds strip small sections off the birch. These beautiful paperlike rolls make wonderful souvenirs. Perhaps you can use one to write your thoughts of the day.

Directions at a glance

0.0   Follow the right ski trail uphill heading northeast (the other trail is marked DO NOT ENTER).

0.05 Turn right (south) on the A, B, and C snowshoe trails signed with bright orange or pink snowshoe silhouette cards.

0.06 Bear right as return loop trail merges from the left.

0.2   Continue straight (south) as the A Trail splits off to the left.

0.3   Bear right (south) as the C Trail and return loop merge from the left. You are beginning a long loop.

2.2   Turn left (west) at a "T" intersection.

2.25 Continue straight (west) as the returning C Trail merges from the right.

2.6   Turn right (north).

2.7   Turn right (east) onto the A and B trails.

2.9   Turn left (west) onto the groomed ski trail. Follow the right-hand trail to the trailhead.

Turning north, the trail begins the most rolling section of the loop. There are six up and down segments of 50 foot elevation or more before you turn west on a more gently rolling trail. The last leg covers some of the outbound trail then loops east, north, and west on gently rolling terrain to return to the trailhead.

How to get there

See "How to get there" on page 147.

Chequamegon Forest Rock Lake 16K Trail
Cable, Wisconsin

Type of trail:	▬▬▬
Also used by:	Snowmobiles cross the trail at several points
Distance:	9.9 miles
Terrain:	Rolling to hilly with some steep sections
Trail difficulty:	Most difficult
Surface quality:	Groomed weekly, single tracked
Food and facilities:	Parking and outdoor toilets are at the trailhead. Winter camping is allowed anywhere except the trailhead parking area. No fee is charged but campers must phone the National Forest Service and camp at least 100 feet from any trail or body of water. Excellent food and lodging are available at Lakewoods Resort, a short distance east of the trailhead, and at Garmisch Resort, 2.5 miles east. All basic services will be found in Cable, 8 miles west.
Fees:	A daily or annual per-vehicle parking fee is required. There is a self-pay station at the trailhead sign board.
Phone numbers:	Cable Area Chamber of Commerce, (800) 533–7454; Chequamegon National Forest, Hayward, (715) 634–4821.
Internet:	www.norwiski.com

The Rock Lake trails are perennial favorites with visitors and local skiers alike. Two decades ago, the National Forest Service chose the scenic, rugged Rock Lake area for its first ski trail in the Chequamegon National Forest. Today the trails retain nearly all of their original character. This is single track, classic cross-country skiing the way it used to be. The trails haven't been widened to accommodate skating or a second track, which makes for an intimate ski experience. Having the trees so close also gives the illusion of greater speed.

There are creature comforts nearby too. Lakewoods Resort is a local favorite for food any time of the day. A modern resort, Lakewoods has an indoor pool and spa. Garmisch, an old lodge with a Bavarian theme, is also known for good food.

The 16K trail is at the low end of the most difficult scale. It mainly gets that rating from its long distance and some tough hills. The terrain is almost constantly rolling and steep grades of 30 to 60 feet are common. A few climbs and descents of 80 to 100 feet will be found. The run-outs on the downhills are pretty straight and shouldn't be a problem unless icy. The trail is always wide enough for a good snowplow.

N

Cha

County Highway M

START/FINISH
Parking

Lakewoods Resort

Twin Lakes

**Chequamegon Forest
Rock Lake 16K Trail**
Scale: 1:33,240 or 1.9" = 1 mile

Hidden Lake

Rock Lake

Emerson Lake

Frels Lake

Birch Lake

nd Lake

McClaine Lake

BAYFIELD CO
SAWYER CO

Spring Lake

Pats Lake

Star Lake

Star Lake

Camp Four Lake

NATIONAL CHEQUAMEGON

Directions at a glance

0.0   From the trailhead sign board at the northeast corner of the parking lot, ski northeast on the groomed ski trail, following light blue diamond markers on trees.

0.75 Continue straight (south) as the 2K Loop turns left.

1.3   Continue straight (south) as the 4K Loop turns left. A few yards beyond, the old road turns left. Continue straight (south).

1.4   Continue straight (south) as the 7.1K Loop turns left.

2.3   Continue straight (west) as the Rock Lake Loop splits off to the right.

2.35 Continue straight (south) as the 11.5K Loop turns left.

4.7   Continue straight (east) across NFR 207.

9.5   Continue straight (northwest) as the 2K Loop merges from the left. Follow to trailhead.

Your ski begins clockwise on the little northern loop then crosses over to go counterclockwise the rest of the way. There are four other loops in the area, 2K, 4K, 7.1K and 11.5K, which turn off and rejoin the 16K trail. They offer possible shortcuts if you find yourself in over your head. All trails are one-way and well marked. There are YOU ARE HERE map signs at trail intersections.

Skiing is pretty easy for the first mile, giving you a nice warm-up. The hills come on as you near Rock Lake. The trail suddenly opens out onto a clear view of the lake. Lined with a mix of hardwoods and pines, Rock Lake is one of the prettiest spots in the forest. There is a ski trail loop that circles the lake, which would add a little over a mile to your ski. Take it on with caution late in the season. The loop has steep grades and the last hill bares up early.

A mile and a half past Rock Lake, a steep downhill run will take you whizzing by the

Skiers love the snow, scenery, and single track classic trails at Rock Lake.

shore of Hildebrand Lake. If you stop for a look, get well off the trail. No one wants to be surprised by a gawking skier in the middle of the trail. Once past Hildebrand Lake the succession of 50-, 70-, and even 100-foot climbs and descents is relentless until you pass the point where the 4K trail merges. After that it's less than 1 mile back to the trailhead.

How to get there
From U.S. 63 in Cable, travel east on County Highway M for 8.2 miles and turn south into the Rock Lake Trails parking lot.

Chequamegon Forest Morgan Falls/St. Peter's Dome Trail
Mellen, Wisconsin

Type of trail:	⬤⬤⬤
Also used by:	Hikers
Distance:	4 miles round-trip
Terrain:	Hilly with very steep sections
Trail difficulty:	Most difficult
Surface quality:	Ungroomed, hiker and snowshoer packed
Food and facilities:	Other than parking, there are no services at the trailhead. All services are available in Ashland, 18 miles north, including outstanding food at the Depot Restaurant and microbrews at the Railyard Pub, both in the restored Soo Line Depot.
Fees:	An annual or daily parking fee is charged. There is a self-pay station at the trailhead.
Phone numbers:	Chequamegon National Forest, (715) 762–2461.
Equipment note:	Use traditional bear paw or modern snowshoes and at least one ski pole.

When local people talk about their favorite places in the Chequamegon National Forest, Morgan Falls and St. Peter's Dome are always near the top of the list. They offer the perfect contrast of experiences.

Morgan Falls is intimate. The state's second highest falls, it tumbles down a rock face in steps. The volume of water is never great, even in spring. In winter the only clue that there is a falls under the snow is an open swirling pool at the base.

On St. Peter's Dome the world opens up. A clear day reveals Lake Superior and the Apostle Islands 20 miles to the north. Below is the vast carpet of the forest and farmsteads in the lowland near the lake. The top

Chequamegon Forest Morgan
Falls/St. Peter's Dome Trail

Scale: 1:17,140 or 3.7" = 1 mile

St. Peters
Dome

Bear
Pond

Morgan Creek

Morgan Falls

Artesian
Well

Parking
START/FINISH

County Line Road

Gravel Pit

Long Lake

BAYFIELD CO
ASHLAND CO
BOUNDARY

FOREST

N

Directions at a glance

0.0 From the southeast corner of the parking lot, at the TO MORGAN FALLS sign, go southeast following small light blue diamond markers on trees.

0.4 Bear right (southeast), staying on the south side of Morgan Creek.

0.6 Turn around at Morgan Falls.

0.8 Turn right (northeast) and immediately cross Morgan Creek. Climb up a short, steep embankment. You should come to a round, stone artesian well.

2.2 Turn around at the St. Peter's Dome overlook.

3.6 Cross Morgan Creek and turn right to return to the trailhead.

is 400 feet above the starting point. St. Peter's is a granite dome created during a billion-year-old mountain building phase that saw huge fissures open in the earth's crust. Molten rock welled up from the mantle, forming features like St. Peter's.

From the parking lot, the trail plunges into a deep woods of maple, balsam, and birch. As the trail meets Morgan Creek, you can look

across and clearly see the trail that leads up to St. Peter's Dome. Don't look for the log bridge described in the Forest Service pamphlet—it was never built. You can visit Morgan Falls first or last. If you are there late in the day, go in first because sunlight fades early in its deep recess.

The climb to the dome begins almost immediately after passing the remnants of an old CCC (Civilian Conservation Corps) camp from the 1930s. All that is visible in winter is the circular stone basin built around an artesian well. The climb is not relentless at first. It begins with a series of ups and downs, with the elevation gains usually greater than the losses.

The vast Chequamegon Forest lies below St. Peter's Dome.

Things get serious in the last 0.5 mile when the final 250 feet are gained. You'll have to handle some real steep pitches to make it to the top. Take some time on St. Peter's Dome to soak up the scenery and sun. After all, snowshoeing shouldn't be all work.

How to get there
From Grand View, go 5 miles north on U.S. 63. Turn right (east) on County Highway E. After 6 miles turn right (south) on County Line Road. Go 4.3 miles and turn left (east) into the Morgan Falls parking lot.

Copper Falls State Park Cascades Trail
Mellen, Wisconsin

Type of trail:	▬▬▬▶
Also used by:	Hikers in some sections
Distance:	3.3 miles
Terrain:	Flat to rolling, and hilly, with some steep sections
Trail difficulty:	Most difficult
Surface quality:	Groomed, single tracked
Food and facilities:	Parking at the trailhead. Outdoor toilets are at the north campground, across the park road from the trailhead and a little north. Indoor shelter and toilets are at the park office/visitor center near the entrance. The visitor center may be open sporadically in winter. Winter camping is available at the north campground; register at the park office.
Fees:	A daily or annual state park pass is required to enter via car. Pay at the entrance booth when open or the self-pay station there.
Phone numbers:	Copper Falls State Park, (715) 274–5123; Mellen Area Chamber of Commerce, (715) 274–2330.

Thousands of years ago, Native Americans mined pure copper ore at Copper Falls. Known as the Copper Culture, they fashioned knives, needles, awls, and projectile points. The Copper Culture were among the first people practicing metallurgy in the world.

There are two falls in the park, Copper and Brownstone. It's the latter you'll get a great view of. Unless the spring melt has begun, the falls will be encased in ice. You'll know the water is flowing by the frothing

Directions at a glance

0.0 From the northeast corner of the trailhead parking lot, ski east on the groomed trail passing a brown-and-white sign that reads VAHTERA SKI TRAIL. These loops lead to Cascades Trail. Follow blue-and-white skier silhouette signs.

0.1 Stay left (east) as the Vahtera Trail turns right.

0.8 Turn left (north) and go 30 yards to the Brownstone Falls overlook platform. Turn around, return to the Cascades Trail and turn left (southeast).

1.0 Turn left (north) immediately after the bridge crossing Tyler Forks.

1.3 Turn right (north) as an ungroomed hiking trail goes straight.

1.7 Turn right (east) as the ungroomed North Country Trail goes straight.

2.3 Turn left (southwest) and cross the bridge over Tyler Forks.

3.2 Stay right (west) as the Vahtera Trail turns left. Follow to trailhead.

pool at the base of the falls. The usual rushing water sound is muted by the ice curtain.

The trail to the falls rolls through a dense forest of hemlock, sugar maple, and birch. Fragrant cedar trees appear as you enjoy an easy, gradual 300-yard run down to the gorge. A few dozen yards north of the trail, an observation platform offers a great view of the Brownstone Falls as it drops 30 feet into a deep gorge. The reddish, sharply fractured rock is hardened lava that once flowed up from fissures in the earth's crust.

A short distance beyond the falls, a bridge across Tyler Forks affords a view of the Cascades upstream. Held tightly in winter's grip, these rapids are mounded with snow. Here and there, open swirling pools dot the snow- and ice-covered scene.

After crossing the river and heading clockwise on the one-way upper loop, the trail rolls for 0.3 mile to a bridge at a small stream. On the other side is the toughest climb of the route. Seventy feet of elevation are gained in just 400 feet of travel. Swinging back to the south, the same elevation is lost in a fun 300-yard downhill run before crossing the little stream again. The single track trail is just wide enough for a good snowplow, with little room for error.

If the Cascades Trail wasn't enough for you, there are three other loops in the park totaling another 10 miles of skiing. Strapping on a pair of snowshoes is a good way to check out the west side of the Bad River and hike to the overlook of Copper Falls.

How to get there
From WI 13, at the north end of Mellen, turn east on WI 169. Go 2 miles to the Copper Falls State Park entrance drive on the left. Follow the drive 1 mile to the winter parking lot.

The roar of Brownstone Falls is silenced by an icy shroud.

Big Bay State Park Trails
La Pointe, Wisconsin

Type of trail: ▬▬ ⬭

Also used by: Hikers

Distance: 5.8 miles round-trip

Terrain: Flat

Trail difficulty: Easy

Surface quality: Ungroomed, skier or snowshoer packed

Food and facilities: Parking at the trailhead. Winter campsites are available in the park. Pay for campsites at the DNR office in Bayfield, 12 miles east on the mainland. Some services are available in La Pointe, 10 miles east, including the Island Cafe where you can get good coffee, soup, and daily specials. All services are available in Bayfield; Maggie's serves great food and good microbrewed beer.

Fees: A daily or annual state park pass is required to enter the park by car. Pay at the DNR office on Third Street in Bayfield or at the self-pay station at the park entrance.

Phone numbers: Big Bay State Park, (715) 779–4020; Apostle Islands National Lakeshore, (715) 779–3397; Bayfield Chamber of Commerce, (800) 447–4094 or (715) 779–3335; Madeline Island Chamber of Commerce, (715) 747–2801 or (888) 475–3386; Trek & Trail, (800) 354–8735.

Internet: www.trek-trail.com

Every part of this easy ski or snowshoe trek is filled with a sense of adventure, even getting to the trail. There is something very fascinating about the Apostle Islands in winter. They are so stark, frozen in the bay's icy grip. Distant islands seem deceptively near. On the Big Bay State Park side of Madeline Island, you can look east across the shore ice to the dark blue expanse of Lake Superior. The lake is so deep it has only frozen over a few times in history. In the distance rise the Porcupine Mountains of Michigan.

It is a good idea to treat this excursion as a real wilderness adventure. Carry a backpack with food and extra clothing, socks, hats, and gloves. Bring fire making supplies, water, a pan to melt snow, a foam pad, and even a sleeping bag if you can fit it. Some of this gear can be stashed along the way to lighten your load. Lake Superior weather can be both unpredictable and treacherous. If you are very hardy, you can camp at designated sites in the park. Otherwise, it is just best to be prepared.

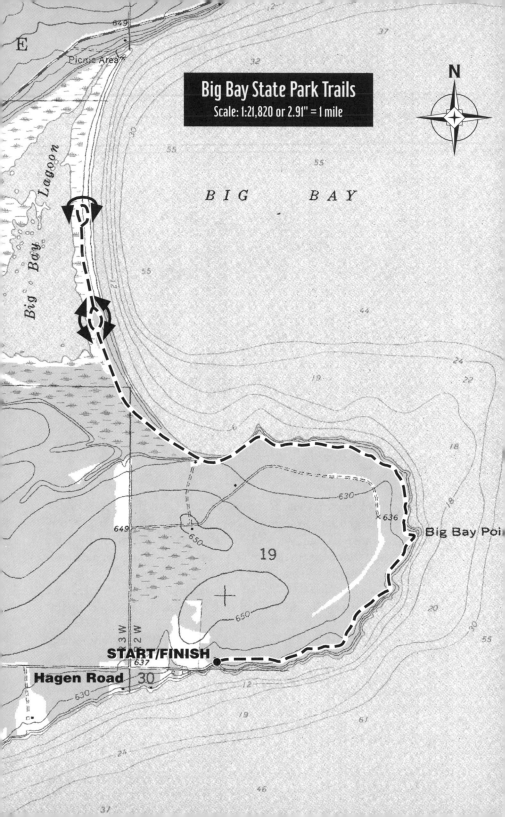

If you come in the hard months of winter, you reach the island via the ice road. It is the only public road on ice in the state—very strange, to say the least. If the day is overcast and gray, the small evergreens that mark the route become extremely important. The road has two-way traffic. Drive on the right side. If there is a white line, you can't see it.

Ferry service begins as soon as possible in late winter. This could be anytime from mid-March to late April. On those early runs the ferry simply smashes a channel like an ice breaker. As it crosses, the ferry rings like a bell as huge slabs of ice slam its hull. The slabs are driven under the boat emerging on the sides like breaching whales.

At the Big Bay State Park trailhead, you can look south over frozen Chequamegon Bay. To the southwest you can spot the smokestacks of the city of Ashland, the last bit of civilization you'll see. The trails are easily followed: You will trace the shoreline first on the Point Trail, then the Bay View Trail, and finally the Nature Trail.

On the first half, the trail snakes through beautiful groves of cedars. The lake is glimpsed through the trees. Some side trails are easily identifiable. Short side trips of a few yards take you to the red sandstone shore on the point. If the lake is acting up, crashing waves put on a show. The falling spray freezes into fantastic ice sculptures.

On cold, quiet days the lake will be frozen for a distance from the shore. You can sit and rest among the ice palaces. The silence is amazing. Once as I sat along the shore, a crow emerged low from just over the cedars. Surprised to find me, it reared up, flaring its wings for a quick direction change. It was so still I could hear the wind in its feathers.

Heading west, you will round a small point. The Bay View Trail opens out on a small cove and the crescent of Big Bay Beach stretches out ahead. Heading to the beach, you'll travel on a boardwalk that normally crosses some boggy stretches. With the bog firmly frozen, you can venture onto it. Perhaps you will spot the green, purple-veined contours of

Directions at a glance

0.0 From the Big Bay Overlook, go east on the Point Trail, following brown-and-white hiker silhouette and trail name signs.

0.3 Continue straight (east) on the Point Trail as the inland Point Trail merges on the left.

0.6 Continue straight (northeast) as the Cut Across Trail turns left.

0.8 Continue straight (northeast) on the Bay View Trail as the Point Trail turns left.

1.9 Bear right (northwest) on the Nature Trail as the Lagoon Ridge Trail splits left.

2.9 Follow the north-end loop around and return to the trailhead.

an insect-eating pitcher plant poking out of the snow. I once found one that had a fly in its frozen pool of fatal liquid.

If the sun is out on a still day, the edge of the bog is a good place to take advantage of all the gear you've brought along. Roll out the foam pad. Jam the snowshoe tails in the snow to make a chair. Pull out those goodies you packed. Sit back and soak up the sun. You'll be amazed at how warm the winter sun can be reflecting off a snow-covered expanse. It's just like a day at the beach.

The final leg of the trail before the turn- around loop traces the narrow sandbar that

The historic trading post at La Pointe is held tight in winter's grip.

separates the bay from an inland lagoon. the return trek is highlighted by views of wooded Big Bay Point across the bay.

You may feel like you've just returned from an Arctic expedition when you get back to Bayfield. If this trip makes you crave more adventure, check out Trek & Trail's multiday dogsled-supported Apostle Island treks. The local outfitter, located on First Street, can take you to the far islands where you can camp in snow caves and marvel at incredible ice formations.

How to get there

From WI 13 in Bayfield, turn east on Washington Avenue and go 0.5 block to either the Madeline Island Ferry dock or the ice road to the island. If on the ice road, follow the traveled route roughly defined by a line of small evergreen trees placed in the ice. When the road reaches land, you are on Whitefish Road. At a "T" intersection turn right on Big Bay Road and follow it around for 0.3 mile to Middle Road (County Highway H) and turn left (east). If you arrive by ferry, turn right at the first intersection off the dock (the Historical Society Museum is straight ahead), go 0.1 mile southeast and turn left (east) on Middle Road (County Highway H).

Follow Middle Road for 3.7 miles to Hagen Road (County Highway H turns left and becomes Black Shanty Road). Continue straight (east) on Hagen Road for 2.2 miles and park at the Bay View Overlook.

Appendix

Ski Centers and Resorts

Afterglow Lake Resort
5050 Sugar Maple Road
P.O. Box 5
Phelps, WI 54554
(715) 545–2560

Bear Paw Inn
N3494 Highway 55
White Lake, WI 54491
(715) 882–3502
Web site: www.bearpawinn.com

High Point Village
W3075 Co. RR
Ogema, WI 54459
(715) 767–5287

Justin Trails
7452 Kathryn Avenue
Sparta, WI 54656
(608) 269–4522 or (800) 488–4521
Web site: www.justintrails.com

Minocqua Winter Park & Nordic
    Center
12375 Scotchman Lake Road
Minocqua, WI 54548
(715) 356–3309

Palmquist's The Farm
N5136 River Road
Brantwood, WI 54513
(715) 564–2558 or (800) 519–2558

The Springs
400 Springs Drive
Spring Green, WI 53588
(608) 588–7000 or (800) 822–7774

Parks and Trail Systems

Apostle Islands National Lakeshore
Route 1, Box 4
Old Courthouse Building
Bayfield, WI 54814
(715) 779–3397

Big Bay State Park
P.O. Box 589
Bayfield, WI 54814
(715) 779–4020

Black River State Forest
910 Highway 54 East
Route 4, Box 18
Black River Falls, WI 54615
(715) 284–1400

Blue Mound State Park
Blue Mounds, WI 53517
(608) 437–5711

Calumet County Parks Department
N6150 County Highway EE
Hilbert, WI 54129
(920) 439–1008

Chequamegon National Forest
1170 Fourth Avenue South
Park Falls, WI 54552
(715) 762–2461

Copper Falls State Park
Box 438
Mellen, WI 54546
(715) 274–5123

Dane County Parks
4318 Robertson Road
Madison, WI 53714
(608) 246–3896

Devils Lake State Park
S5975 Park Road
Baraboo, WI 53913-9299
(608) 356–8301

Interstate State Park
Box 703
St. Croix Falls, WI 54024
(715) 483–3747

Kettle Moraine State Forest,
    Lapham Peak Unit
N846 W329 County Highway C
Delafield, WI 53018
(414) 646–3025

Kettle Moraine State Forest,
    Northern Unit
Box 410
Campbellsport, WI 53010
(414) 626–2116

Kettle Moraine State Forest,
    Southern Unit
S91 W39091 Highway 59
Eagle, WI 53119
(414) 594–2135

Marathon County Forestry
    Department
500 Forest Street
Wausau, WI 54403
(715) 847–5267

Marathon County Park Department
Courthouse
Wausau, WI 54401-5568
(715) 847–5235

National Forest Service
Route 10, Box 508
Hayward, WI 54843
(715) 634–4821

Old World Wisconsin
S103 W37890 Highway 67
Eagle, WI 53119
(414) 594–6300
Web site: oww.shsw.wisc.edu/

Perrot State Park
Route 1, Box 407
Trempealeau, WI 54661
(608) 534–6409

Portage County Parks Department
Portage County Courthouse
1516 Church Street
Stevens Point, WI 54481
(715) 346–1433

Potawatomi State Park
3740 Park Drive
Sturgeon Bay, WI 54235
(920) 746–2890

Wisconsin Department of Natural
    Resources
Bureau of Parks and Recreation
P.O. Box 7921
Madison, WI 53707-7921
(608) 266–2181

Wyalusing State Park
13342 County Highway C
Bagley, WI 53801
(608) 996–2261

Area Information

Antigo Area Chamber of Commerce
P.O. Box 339
Antigo, WI 54409
(715) 623–4134 or (888) 526–4523
Web site: www.newnorth.net/
    antigo.chamber

Baraboo Area Chamber of
    Commerce
P.O. Box 442
Baraboo, WI 53913
(800) 227–2266
E-mail: chamber@baraboo.com

Bayfield Chamber of Commerce
P.O. Box 138
Bayfield, WI 54814-0138
(800) 447–4094 or (715) 779–3335
E-mail: bayfield@win.bright.net

Black River Area Chamber of
    Commerce
336 North Water Street
Black River Falls, WI 54615
(715) 284–4658

Cable Area Chamber of Commerce
P.O. Box 217
Cable, WI 54821
(800) 533–7454
E-mail: gocable@win.bright.net

Cambridge Chamber of Commerce
P.O. Box 330
Cambridge, WI 53523-0330
(608) 423–3780
Web site: www.cambridgewi.com

Chippewa Valley Convention and
  Visitors Bureau
3625 Gateway Drive
Suite F
Eau Claire, WI 54701
(888) 523–FUNN

Door County Chamber of
  Commerce
P.O. Box 40
Sturgeon Bay, WI 54235
(920) 743–4456
Web site: www.
  doorcountyvacations.com

Fox Cities Convention and Visitors
  Bureau
110 Fox River Drive
Appleton, WI 54915-9108
(920) 734–3356
E-mail: tourism@foxcities.org

Hayward Area Chamber of
  Commerce
P.O. Box 726
Hayward, WI 54843-0726
(800) 724–2992 or (715) 634–8662
E-mail: hayward@win.bright.net

Madeline Island Chamber of
  Commerce
P.O. Box 274
La Pointe, WI 54850-0274
(715) 747–2801
Web site: www.madelineisland.
  com

Manitowoc–Two Rivers Area
  Chamber of Commerce
P.O. Box 903
Manitowoc, WI 54421-0903
(800) 262–7892 or (414) 684–5575
Web site: www.mtwctrchamber.com

Mellen Area Chamber of Commerce
P.O. Box 793
Mellen, WI 54546
(715) 274–2330

Minocqua–Arbor Vitae–Woodruff
  Area Chamber of Commerce
P.O. Box 1006-W
Minocqua, WI 54548
(715) 356–5266 or (800) 446–6784
Web site: www.minocqua.org

Oconomowoc Bureau of Tourism
P.O. Box 27
Oconomowoc, WI 53066
(414) 569–2185
E-mail: info@ci.oconomowoc.wi.us

Phelps Chamber of Commerce
P.O. Box 217
Phelps, WI 54554
(715) 545–3800

Plymouth Chamber of Commerce
P.O. Box 584
Plymouth, WI 53073-0584
(920) 893–0079 or (888) 693–8263
E-mail: plymouthchamber@excel.net

Polk County Information Center
710 Highway 35 South
St. Croix Falls, WI 54024
(715) 483–1410 or (800) 222–POLK
Web site: www.obnet.com/
  polk-county/tourism/

Prairie du Chien Tourism Council
P.O. Box 326
Prairie du Chien, WI 53821
(608) 326–8555 or (800) PDC–1673
E-mail: pdcoc@mhtc.net

Price County Tourism Department
Price County Courthouse
126 Cherry Street
Phillips, WI 54555-1249
(800) 269–4505 or (715) 339–4505

Rib Lake Commercial & Civic Club
P.O. Box 205
Rib Lake, WI 54470
(715) 427–5761 or (800) 819–5253

Sheboygan County Convention
  and Visitors Bureau
712 Riverfront Drive, Suite 101
Sheboygan, WI 53081-4665
(800) 457–9497, ext 500 or (920)
  457–9495
Web site: www.sheboygan.com

Spring Green Chamber of
  Commerce
P.O. Box 3
Spring Green, WI 53588
(608) 588–2042 or (800) 588–2042
Web site: www.execpc.com/~spring

Stevens Point Chamber of
  Commerce
600 Main Street
Stevens Point, WI 54481
(715) 344–1940 or (800) 236–4636
E-mail: spacvb@coredcs.com

Taylor County Tourism Council
P.O. Box 172
Medford, WI 54451
(800) 257–4729 or (715) 748–4729

Tomahawk Chamber of Commerce
P.O. Box 412
Tomahawk, WI 54487
(715) 453–5334 or (800) 569–2160
E-mail: tmhwkcoc@newnorth.net

Trempealeau County Clerk's Office
1720 Main Street
Whitehall, WI 54773
(715) 538–2311 or (800) 927–5339

Waupaca Area Chamber of
  Commerce
221 South Main Street
Waupaca, WI 54981
(715) 258–7343 or (888) 417–4040
E-mail: discoverwaupaca@
  waupacaareachamber.com

Wausau/Central Wisconsin
  Convention and Visitors Council
10101 Market Street
Suite B20
Mosinee, WI 54455
(715) 355–8788 or (888) 948–4748
E-mail: cwcvb@dwave.net

Whitewater Area Chamber of
  Commerce
P.O. Box 34
Whitewater, WI 53190-0034
(414) 473–4005 or (414) 473–0520
E-mail: wacc@idcnet.com

Useful Publications and Web Sites

American Birkebeiner
www.birkie.org

BASTA—Brown County Area Ski
Trail Association, Green Bay
www.basta.org

Bruce Adelsman's Cross-Country
Ski Page
www.skinnyski.com

Cross Country Skiing in Northwest
Wisconsin
www.norwiski.com

Madnordski—Nordic Skiing in
Wisconsin
danenet.wicip.org/madnord

Silent Sports magazine
P.O. Box 152
Waupaca, WI 54981
(715) 258–5546;

E-mail: wpcompany@aol.com
Provides the most complete calen-
dar of events

Wausau Nordic Ski Club
www.dwave.net/~keester/
wausaunordic.htm

Wisconsin Fall/Winter Event &
Recreation Guide
Free from the Wisconsin
Department of Tourism
(800) 432–8747
www.tourism.state.wi.us

Wisconsin Nordic Network
www.skiwisconsin.com

About the Author

Phil Van Valkenberg has loved skiing all his life. He doubts he could ever live in a place where winter didn't mean snow. The first snowfall is always a time of joy for him. Phil has skied a marathon-distance cross-country ski race every winter for twenty-four years, including twenty-two American Birkebeiner races. Comparatively, he is a latecomer to snowshoeing, participating in the sport for twenty years. He loves the new modern-design snowshoes.

This is Phil's first winter trails book. He has authored six books on bicycling, including *Best Bike Rides® Midwest*. He lives by a quiet lake near Cambridge, Wisconsin.